Sacred Summer

Sacred Summer

A Mom's Guide to Resilience, Discovery, and Family Fun

Risa Seelenfreund

Columbus, Ohio

Sacred Summer: A Mom's Guide to Resilience, Discovery, and Family Fun

Published by Gatekeeper Press
2167 Stringtown Rd, Suite 109
Columbus, OH 43123-2989
www.GatekeeperPress.com

Copyright © 2021 by Risa Seelenfreund

All rights reserved. Neither this book, nor any parts within it may be sold or reproduced in any form or by any electronic or mechanical means, including information storage and retrieval systems without permission in writing from the author. The only exception is by a reviewer, who may quote short excerpts in a review.

The editorial work for this book is entirely the product of the author. Gatekeeper Press did not participate in and is not responsible for any aspect of this element.

Library of Congress Control Number: 2021933678

ISBN (paperback): 9781662908200
eISBN: 9781662908217

For David:
For loving me, believing in me,
and letting me be me.

Contents

Introduction	1
Month One: Settling into an Unconventional Summer	5
Month Two: The Stresses and Rewards of the Strangest Summer Ever	43
Month Three: Finding Peace	103
Afterword	152
Helpful Links	154
Family Activity List	155
Getting Started on Your Resilience Journey: Exercises to Apply the COPAP Model to Your Own Life	159
• COPAP Lesson of the Day Writing Practice	160
• Learning from Past Experiences	162
• Control: Distinguishing Between What You Can and Cannot Control	164
• Opportunity: Changing Your Perspective	166
• Purpose: Identifying Your Reason for Being	168
• Attitude of Gratitude: Finding Something to Be Grateful For	171
• Play: Doing Something You Love	173
• Resilience for Kids	175
Acknowledgements	183

Exercises, bonus resources, and our summer in color available at www.sacredsummerbook.com.

Introduction

Resilience. It's a word that gets thrown around a lot during difficult times.

I'm fascinated with resilience. It's my jam. I teach, coach, and speak about resilience. I love helping people better manage the difficulties they face in life. Helping in even a small way gets me energized about my career choice.

Until now, the examples I've shared in my work were usually *other* people's difficulties and tragedies, rarely my own. Revealing my own vulnerabilities was too uncomfortable. Besides, who would be interested in *my* troubles?

Then March 2020 arrived. COVID19 hit my neighborhood … early and hard. Everything shut down fast and people retreated to their own bubbles, desperately trying to remain healthy and safe.

Overnight, needing resilience (and sanitizer and toilet paper) became universal. I began to feel connected to humanity in ways I had never felt before. Together we were coping with the long haul of a pandemic: anxieties about illness, worries about work, virtual school, no summer camp, and the whole host of other concerns that came with our new circumstances.

In earnest, I focused on utilizing my own tools for building resilience and found them infinitely helpful. I knew I had a story to tell and help to offer.

To back up a minute, let me define resilience. In a nutshell, resilience is the ability to bounce back from a difficult situation. Think of resilience as a rubber band. You can stretch, bend, twist, and stress it and it will still bounce back. That's resilience: getting bent out of shape and having the capacity to rebound.

To be sure, having resilience doesn't mean bouncing back will be easy. That's where resilience tools come in. These tools can help make bouncing back significantly easier, with less stress and suffering.

I call my resilience model COPAP. All my tools and worksheets stem from this model. My own growth comes from applying this model. The letters in COPAP stand for:

- **C**ontrol: Distinguish between what you can and cannot control. Let go of things you cannot control and focus your energy on changing those things you *can* control.

- **O**pportunity: Changes can be viewed in different lights. Work on seeing changes positively—as opportunities to learn something new, try something a new way, or give up something that wasn't working well for you anyway.

- **P**urpose: Everyone has a reason for being. You may not have discovered yours yet. Take the time to do so, then use your purpose as a reason to get up and get going every day.

- **A**ttitude of Gratitude: While it may be hard to feel grateful when things are tough, there is always something that could be worse. Be thankful for what you *do* have, and grateful that things are no worse than they are.

- **P**lay: Have fun! Take the time to do things you love, whether individually or with others.

As I worked on using COPAP to build my own resilience, I began thinking, "Couldn't others benefit from my experiences and tools?" Hmm. Maybe sharing my troubles and solutions could help others with similar challenges.

At the same time I worked on building my resilience, I was approached by many people who encouraged me to share the numerous family activities that we engaged in to stay busy and entertained during this bizarre summer. This book includes several of these pursuits as well as an activity list as a reference. I strongly believe they enhanced my family's relationship with one another, as well as increased our ability to cope.

What follows is a series of journal entries that I adapted into vignettes (all are true!). I wrote them over twelve weeks during the summer of 2020 as I worked to increase my resilience (and keep my kids busy, maintain my sanity, and keep my sense of humor). Most important, each vignette ends with the lessons I learned from my experiences that day. Some lessons are simple, some more profound, but each is a window into my growth.

This intentional writing practice turned that intensely difficult summer into a sacred, precious experience that had a deep impact on my life. I hope that by reading my entries, you feel inspired to take up a similar practice that in turn profoundly impacts your life.

To set expectations: I did not have to endure tragedy during those trying summer months. I don't pretend that my experiences are comparable to those who lost loved ones or struggled to put food on the table. Nevertheless, I struggled in my own way, and resilience helped me cope with my day-to-day challenges. Resilience is not restricted to catastrophe. Whether managing tragedy or more mundane woes, building resilience can help make handling life, and the difficulties it throws at you, a little bit easier. Who knows, you may even find some joy and fun along the way.

Note: names have been changed to protect the innocent and not-so-innocent.

MONTH ONE: SETTLING INTO AN UNCONVENTIONAL SUMMER

Camp Counselor (or Cruise Director?)

Today was the last day of the school year. I say that half-jokingly because virtual school petered out after Memorial Day. By 10:00 this morning, school was done for Liam (12 years old) and Chloe (10 years old). It was officially summer vacation.

Hurray? The kids were certainly happy, though more subdued than they usually are at the end of a normal school year. Me, I have mixed feelings. I'll miss the structure (and quiet) school provided for at least part of the day. But I'm happy for the children that the challenge of virtual school is over—at least for the next few months.

Along with the end of school comes my shift in responsibility from homeschool teacher to camp counselor. Or maybe I should think of myself as a cruise director. Ooh, that sounds fun. Remember Julie McCoy? With the kids' in-person camps cancelled and face-to-face activities discouraged, it falls on me to find ways to keep Liam and Chloe engaged and entertained. In a way, it sounds fun. And I've certainly bought enough indoor and outdoor activities to make it *seem* fun.

The question is how am I going to work and play counselor all summer? The answer to that question is a mystery. My consulting business is slow right now, so, for the moment, I have the chance to spend my time as an energetic and cheery counselor. With luck, this free time won't be around too long though.

What is not a mystery is my purpose. I am clear that I was put on this earth to do two things: help and teach. As I think about how to keep my kids busy, my business afloat, and my family happy, I remain dedicated to achieving my purpose. It will get me up every morning and keep me going through each day. I will find ways to continue teaching through my business. (Though, frankly, it will take some creativity because in the current climate my clients have neither the budget nor wherewithal to focus on refining their leadership behaviors or team building skills.) And, I am determined to engage my children in new learning opportunities, whatever those might look like this summer. It will be a challenge, no doubt, but my purpose will drive me during this unconventional time.

My other noteworthy struggle this summer? Managing my anxiety over COVID. Ordinary illnesses already make me slightly nuts; a new, unknown virus with significant death rates is making me a legitimate nervous wreck. Sigh.

COPAP Lesson of the Day

- Our family is usually incredibly busy. This summer is creating a chance for us to pause, slow down, and enjoy spending time together. Not a bad opportunity.

King Cone

Grandma and Grandpa dropped by this afternoon. We took our usual seats in the front yard, our lawn furniture placed a socially-distanced ten feet apart. Thankfully, no gardeners were in the neighborhood blasting their lawnmowers, making conversation with the 80 year old grandparents impossible.

At one point, we did hear the melodious tones of an ice cream truck in the neighborhood. Woohoo! This sound was particularly significant for Liam and Chloe because just the day before we'd made the decision to start buying ice cream from the truck (one of the benefits of our county approaching "Phase III" of its COVID re-opening plan).

Over the past few weeks, every time the kids heard the truck, my husband and I were met with sad, pleading eyes despite our decision that we would not stand on a crowded line or get close to the ice cream server who did not wear a mask.

Now that the time had come to dip our toes into the delight of summer ice cream vendors, the kids were ecstatic, truly over the moon, to hear the familiar, tinkly music. I grabbed my mask and ran down the street with Liam like a crazy woman. Sadly, the truck had turned in the opposite direction and, despite our outrageous gesticulations, did not head back our way.

The children were utterly dejected. Life had ended for want of a King Cone. Mind you, it's not as if they've been deprived of the pleasures of frozen snacks. They've eaten gobs of ice cream from our own freezer for months. But, to be fair, there was some sense to their sadness. So much had been taken from them during the past three months. The King Cone was the perfect metaphor for the royal pain this pandemic had become.

I sent the kids inside to make themselves ice cream cones. They were only half excited by this consolation prize.

We offered Grandpa a cone too. How could he resist? Liam came out a few minutes later with Grandpa's vanilla cone. How do we overcome the monumental challenge of getting the cone to Grandpa while social distancing? We could toss it. Put it on a long stick. Leave it on a lawn chair for Grandpa to retrieve. Too preposterous. I stretched out my arm, he stretched his, and we managed to do the transfer. Strange how coming within a couple feet of my dad felt as if we were living life on the edge.

Such is life these days. It's been over 100 days since I've hugged or kissed my parents or even seen them indoors. I'm grateful to spend time with them, but I so miss being able to invite them into my home.

On a lighter note, the Slip 'N Slide I ordered five weeks ago miraculously arrived today. Hooray! One activity taken care of. We hooked it up, and the kids took a cool glide down 30 feet of wet, splashy bliss. An irritating thought came to me after we'd spent what felt like hours in the afternoon sun setting up the darn thing ... we would have to take it down every time we used it. The prospect of daily cleanup suddenly diminished the Slip 'N Slide's initial appeal.

As for the enjoyment factor of the new slide, Chloe was captivated. She was a happy, giggly 10-year-old, running, sliding, and going back for more again and again. Liam enjoyed it for a while, but then complained he was getting "too wet."

It's going to be a long summer.

COPAP Lessons of the Day

- I can't control the ice cream truck, but I can offer ice cream from our freezer. A simple but good lesson in finding alternatives when things don't go our way.
- Play is not the same for everyone, and that's okay.

Wheeeee!

Transverse Myelitis

It's tough having a child with health issues. I couldn't fully appreciate this challenge until two and a half years ago when Chloe suddenly got very sick and wound up in the hospital, paralyzed from the waist down. She had a neurological illness called transverse myelitis. It sure makes you appreciate everything about your child ... their loveliness, their quirks, their exasperating behaviors, *everything*, when they fall significantly ill.

We are lucky that Chloe has recovered—mostly. Thankfully, she can walk, run, and play with her friends. She looks like a typical 10-year-old. What people don't see is that her bladder never fully recovered from the paralysis, and she continues to have significant bladder issues.

The trauma has left our whole family with emotional scars. Chloe is plagued by questions about why this happened to her, and why the physical manifestations won't go away. Liam has to deal with Mom and Dad sometimes prioritizing his sister's needs over his. And Dan and I constantly worry about Chloe's well-being.

When COVID hit, I worried. *Really* worried. The possibility of anyone in my family getting very sick was extremely difficult to bear. I know that our family's past trauma is influencing how I'm dealing with COVID today. My perspective is skewed by my previous experiences, and those experiences have left me battered as a parent.

So, while others may choose to "pod" with other families or indulge in dinners at restaurants, we do not. Our summer may be restricted, but it's what we need to do to maintain our sanity and sense of control around our children's health.

COPAP Lesson of the Day

- I'm finding it hard to deal with the lack of control around COVID. I know I'm impacted by my past experiences with Chloe. This awareness can help me distinguish between what I can and can't control and allow me to focus on things I can influence like spending quality time with my family.

Orange (Nope, Clementine) Chicken

I was busy with work today, surprising for a summer Friday, and thoroughly shocking given the way COVID has slowed my business, but I'm thrilled to have a project to work on.

I had no time today to occupy the kids, so there was a lot of TV, some video games, but also some basketball and dice games with Dad. He does know how to entertain them. I'm not sure how thrilled I am with their playing college dice games, but it's better than a full day of TV, right? Maybe so? I just don't know what's best this summer.

I stepped out of our home office midday to have lunch. I asked the family if they wanted to join me. When their movie was over, they said. Seriously, a movie at noon on a beautiful summer day? Ugh.

When they were ready for lunch, they wanted to make homemade pizza. Sounded fine, but guess who stretched the dough, cut the fresh mozzarella, and plucked the basil from our new, organic basil plant? Not the kids on summer break. Nope. I prepped the pizza and left them to cook and eat it while I got on a business call. Note to self: this division of labor must change. It's definitely not working for me.

The rest of the afternoon rolled on. Chloe took an online class where she created her own planet. Bless her little mind, this girl is fascinated with astronomy. Her planet had a ring, water, land, and other innovative planetary features that I can't name. One very well spent, screen-filled hour.

Before dinner, Chloe decided to use the Slip 'N Slide again. We went through the whole set up and cleanup process a little faster than last time. I'm hoping we'll get the whole procedure down to a science before the kids get bored of the whole thing.

Liam decided not to engage, what with the horror of getting wet and all.

Though not a Slip 'N Slide enthusiast, Liam is a great help in the kitchen. Earlier in the day he requested orange chicken for dinner. It's his favorite meal at our go-to Asian fusion restaurant, where we haven't been for over three months. "Why not?" I thought. It would be a nice treat for us all. I looked online and, to Liam's chagrin, found a healthy orange chicken recipe. Because this was a last-minute choice, and we're avoiding unnecessary trips to the grocery store, we had to rely on ingredients we had on hand. While we didn't have a single orange, we did have a boatload of clementines. And, so, I morphed our dish into clementine chicken. It didn't take long to learn it's a pain in the neck to zest a clementine. We also learned that healthy clementine chicken is not tasty. To be perfectly accurate, it's awful. We discarded the sauce and used bottled teriyaki instead. So much for homemade and healthy.

The highlight of my day came after dinner. We left Dan home to clean up, and the kids and I went for an unbelievably pleasant bike ride. After a hot, humid day, it had cooled down and a slight breeze had picked up. After a busy work and mom-camp day, it was relaxing and mind-clearing. Don't get me wrong, I was a sweaty, panting mess, but I truly loved it and returned home in a great frame of mind. I felt so grateful for a lovely evening and a husband who cleans up dinner.

COPAP Lessons of the Day

- Be grateful for both the big and little things: work, Chloe's interest in astronomy, Liam's help with cooking, Dan's help with cleaning, a beautiful evening.
- Embrace whatever play means to each member of my family. Maybe our interests will align, maybe not. It doesn't matter as long as we all take the time to play in a way that makes us each feel happy and fulfilled.

Family Cooking Competition, Part Deux

A few weeks ago we decided to start a family cooking challenge. The only requirements were that the meal had to be meatless (fish was deemed acceptable) and include a main dish and a side. Anything else was fair game. We were so professional, we even created a rubric to measure success: We would be measured on flavor, cook, presentation, and creativity.

We split into teams—Chloe and me against Liam and Dan. Chloe and I presented our dinner last weekend: homemade biscuits with chive butter, cod in a butter and lemon sauce, mashed potatoes, and roasted broccoli (yes, butter is our friend). It was delicious, and we were exceedingly proud of ourselves.

Tonight was Liam and Dan's chance to shine. And, boy, did they ever surprise us. They shone brighter than we'd imagined they could. They scored higher than Chloe and I did. As the regular chef in the house, I was more than a bit humiliated. They made cod parmesan, sautéed broccoli, angel hair, and fresh, hot, homemade bread. Wow. I admit I underestimated their capabilities, especially Dan's given the limited amount of time he spends in the kitchen. Clearly, he needs to be reintroduced to this critical room in our house. But he'd better not cook fish parmesan, biscuits, and mashed potatoes on a regular basis, or we'll be too huge to run for the next ice cream truck.

This exercise was great for us. Creative, fun, educational, and good family bonding. We've made the decision to continue these competitions throughout the summer. Next up: desserts. OMG. More butter.

I ended the evening by attending a Zoom call to honor World Refugee Day. Former refugees and their families shared harrowing stories of their ordeals. Now, there's a way to ground you.

COPAP Lessons of the Day

- While I can't control the pandemic, I can control what I do to keep my family busy and entertained (and eat good food in the process).

- There's no better way to put my petty concerns into perspective than to hear moving stories about truly difficult situations. Forget my complaints about Slip 'N Slides, butter, and being shown up as a cook. I'm truly grateful.

- It's not camp, but cooking yummy food as a family is a great way to play.

Bon appétit

Cupcakes

Today is Father's Day!

We had a fun day celebrating Dan and the grandfathers. For the first time since COVID hit, we had family over in the backyard. Until now, we've sat in the driveway separated by well over six feet. Afraid that guests would breathe too close to our house, we sat them at the edge of our property. (Okay, a bit of an exaggeration, but not entirely untrue.)

But, today, we welcomed them into the glory of our shady backyard. They sat at one end of our six-foot-long table (yup, I measured to be sure), and we sat at the other. How nice to be together in the relative privacy of our yard instead of our public front yard in full view of dogwalkers, gardeners, and ever-present Amazon delivery workers.

We even ate together. My sister, Abby, and I have birthdays coming up in the next couple of days, so to celebrate I baked. Thinking it would involve less communal touching, I made cupcakes so I could hand each person an individual portion with a long pair of tongs. Brilliant, I thought. Exceptional times call for unique solutions.

I joke, but it's difficult to see my parents and sister from such a distance. No hugging, no kissing, no touching at all. It's taking an emotional toll.

On a happy note, I'm thrilled to report that the Slip 'N Slide got considerable use today. It was a hot, muggy day, and the kids were bored talking with the adults, so they slipped and they slid—and not a single complaint.

COPAP Lessons of the Day

- A simple reminder to take opportunities to celebrate the good things, especially during difficult times.
- Eat cupcakes! They make most things better.

Half a Century

Today is my birthday! And a BIG one it is. It's been hard to come to terms with turning 50. While people keep telling me it's just a number, it's difficult to think of the number in a positive light when my children keep reminding me that I'm half a century. Wow, that sounds old.

Despite thoughts of becoming an old lady, I've had a fabulous day. Yesterday I went to bed feeling disappointed that I'd have to celebrate my 50th birthday at home instead of in Europe on the fantastic trip we'd planned, but today has turned out perfectly. Dan organized a day of virtual and in-person (socially-distant, of course) visits from friends and family. I spent the entire day going from appointment to appointment, celebrating and catching up with important people in my life in New York, Chicago, Texas, Florida, California, Colorado, and even Malaysia. Under normal, non-COVID circumstances, these chats never would have happened, and I'm grateful for the way my day turned out.

We even ordered in food for the first time since early March. Even better than the delicious food was not having to cook or clean up the kitchen. I've been cooking and cleaning every evening for over 100 days, so take-out was an exceptional treat.

I'm also exceedingly grateful for Dan, who created the experience for me. (I'm even thankful for the gluten-free peanut butter cake concoction that, bless his heart, he attempted to bake.) I know that I'm loved, and it feels good.

COPAP Lessons of the Day

- I need to take opportunities to speak with important people in my life. It brings me so much joy.

- Play doesn't have to be complicated and exotic to be worthwhile. The day wasn't the "play" I had hoped for, but play I did, and I loved it!

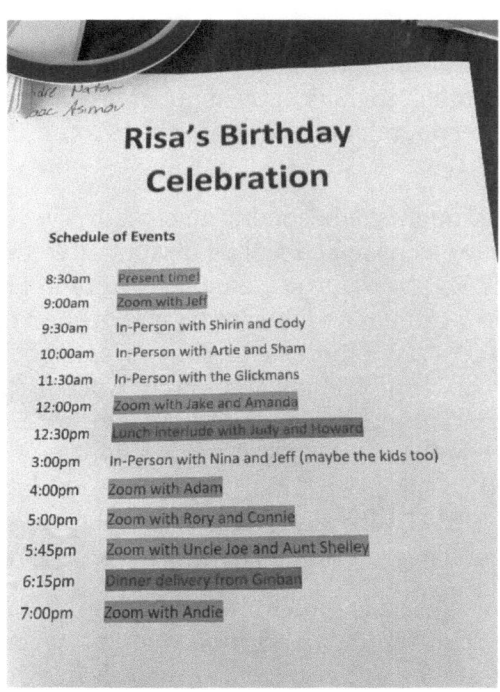

My busy birthday schedule

Peer Pressure

Today, Phase III of our county's re-opening begins. Yay! I can get a tattoo.

I ended the day with my Tuesday Ladies Zoom call. It's a weekly call with some local women where we catch up and sometimes play an online game, but mostly we chat. We talk about life, kids, and how we're handling the new normal.

Being an introvert, I don't often hang out with friends during normal times, but now I have a weekly call to socialize. It's a nice side effect of this difficult situation. Next week, we're planning for an outdoor, socially distant get-together. I'm excited but a bit nervous and hesitant. Will others observe social distancing? Will they wear masks? Will I feel pressured to do something I'm not comfortable with? The questions, the stress. I feel like a teenager again.

COPAP Lesson of the Day

- Opportunities aren't always easy to take on and may cause some stress. I need to decide if the angst is worth it. In this case, I think it is.

Purpose

Today I recorded one of my "micro learning episodes" for work. Because my business has slowed considerably since March, I'm trying to stay busy and relevant. I'm recording 5-minute training videos on everything from building resilience, to strategies for working effectively from home, to race in the workplace (inspired by the death of George Floyd and the ensuing protests), to leading during a crisis.

Recording myself all alone is a strange thing. I'm perfectly comfortable facilitating in front of a live audience. It's an entirely different animal when I'm teaching in front of a roomful of nobody. I miss the give and take of an engaged group.

At least Liam is involved. He helps me edit and post on YouTube. Yay! An activity for him and a partner for me.

This project is time-consuming and a little lonely, but it aligns with my purpose to teach and help, so it keeps me going when I'm feeling discouraged.

COPAP Lessons of the Day

- I'm grateful to have time to sit back and reflect on my purpose. I know frontline workers are working their butts off right now and barely have time to breathe, let alone reflect.

- Fulfilling my purpose isn't always quick and easy. That's okay. It's totally worth the effort.

- My purpose doesn't have to be fulfilled alone. I can engage family to play while I pursue my purpose. A win-win.

105

This evening I checked my Facebook feed. Here's what I saw, "Just in case you lost count, today is Day 105, Week 15" of shutdown from COVID19. I also saw a post with a friend's family photo and the caption, "Our replacement summer." What a long, strange summer it will be.

COPAP Lesson of the Day

- Summer isn't gone, it's just different. We have the opportunity to replace it with something new and unconventional. This change doesn't have to mean something bad.

A reminder we didn't need

Snip, Snip

The time has come. It's been over three months since COVID shut down New York. That bit of info means I've skipped the hair salon for far too long. A couple weeks ago I finally broke down and bought bottled hair dye because I could not stand looking at my grays another minute. I was determined to celebrate my 50th birthday with a head of brown hair. A haircut, though—*that* I was not willing to experiment with on my own.

Until today. I could take it no longer. My mop was long, thick, and itchy. You could barely make out my small face among the massive waves of curls.

There was no way I could do the cut myself with all those layers and curls. I had to recruit Dan. Lord help us. We went outside to avoid a mountain of curls on our bathroom floor (I had already experienced that delightful clean-up with the other family members' cuts), and he began to snip, snip, snip away. I felt as if each snip was like a pin going into a voodoo doll of my hairdresser. The poor woman was probably feeling a stabbing pain with each uneven clip of the scissors.

On the bright side, the beauty of curly hair is that it's more forgiving of bad haircuts than straight hair.

COPAP Lessons of the Day

- Annoyances can become godsends. I'm finally grateful for my curly mop!
- I'm also thankful I have no glamorous galas or photo shoots to attend any time in the near future (or, well, ever).

I feel pretty...oh so pretty!

Taking the Plunge

At 7:00, Dan and I were up and out of bed. Why so early on a Saturday? Why so early on *any* morning, really, when we've had no place to go for the past 105+ days? Well, because today we had someplace to go! We had a 9:00 a.m. reservation at a local ropes park. We were going to climb and swing through the trees.

An obsessive amount of thought went into making this reservation. The main impetus was the family membership we bought for the holidays back in December, a lifetime ago. When we got the membership, we had visions of climbing as a family once a week from April through November. We'd bond, we'd work out, we'd be a family of Tarzans and Janes. How exciting. How athletic. How outdoorsy!

COVID nixed that ambitious dream. The ropes park remained shuttered through April and May and halfway through the month of June. It finally opened two weeks ago. Thus began our decision-making process of whether or not we felt it was safe to go. We were eager to climb but also hesitant. The course established safety protocols, but would people abide by them? Would climbers wear masks when off the ropes and distance themselves when on them? How would we be harnessed by staff members while social distancing? Would the restrooms be clean and empty? AAAKKKK! I wanted to be the fun, brave, not-a-care-in-the-world mom—but I just wasn't.

In the end, Dan and I decided to take the plunge (metaphorically speaking, of course). We reasoned that we'd be outdoors, breathing fresh air, with a limited number of other climbers. We knew we could leave any time we felt uncomfortable or unsafe. Even so, I was nervous and felt as if I were putting our family at risk.

Laden with concern and safety supplies, we headed out the door. Before starting the car, Dan checked his phone. A heavy groan emanated from deep in his throat. In a moment of impeccable timing, he got a message from the ropes park announcing they were closing for the day due to impending thunderstorms.

All that angst and prep—wasted. I can't say that a part of me wasn't relieved (overjoyed?) that the option to go was taken from us, but I was also disappointed. We had finally worked up the nerve to do an activity outside the house and, in the blink of an eye, the opportunity was gone.

Oh, and with incredible irony, the thunderstorms never materialized.

COPAP Lesson of the Day

- This was one of those situations that was out of my control. Whatever my feelings about it, there was nothing I could do to change it. The good news? I can always try again. *That's* within my control.

Camp Night

The rain finally arrived.

The kids have been so sad that sleep-away camp was cancelled that I decided to bring a bit of camp to them. We'd planned to barbeque, tell ghost stories, and have outdoor fun, just as they would have done at camp. Well, not JUST like camp, but we were hoping to re-create a similar experience.

The rain wouldn't stop *this* mom from delivering fun for her cubs! We still barbequed hot dogs and hamburgers, grilled corn, and ate watermelon. No healthy grilled chicken and veggies on this night. This was camp night! We chowed down indoors at our kitchen table instead of outside, but we simulated the best we could. Ghost stories? No problem, we brought a tent into the living room and told scary stories with a flashlight.

And what's camp night without s'mores? Liam and I were ready to deliver.

Cooking Competition: Dessert Edition began today. Liam and I went all out. We made s'mores completely from scratch. Homemade graham crackers, handmade chocolate, and custom-made marshmallows. We spent hours (I'm not kidding ... *four* hours) creating our delightful masterpiece. (And you should have seen the not-so-delightful kitchen after those four hours.)

Admittedly, the final result was a little off ... graham crackers a little too thick, dark chocolate a little too bitter, and marshmallows a little too mushy. Still, it was great fun to create this quintessential summertime treat with my boy and be able to share it with my family, even indoors.

COPAP Lesson of the Day

- Today I thought of the old saying about learning to dance in the rain. We can't control the weather, but we can still play indoors, have plenty of fun, and dance despite the rain.

Sacred Summer

Can I have s'more?

Spooky!

Road Trip!

Sadly, not for vacation. Why, you might ask, did we take a road trip if not for fun, especially to the glorious city of Wilmington, Delaware? (No offense, Joe Biden.) Well, Chloe had surgery at the children's hospital there in February and because of COVID we hadn't been able to go back for a follow-up visit.

This month, they started seeing non-emergency patients again. Because the hospital would let in only one parent with a child, we decided that one parent would stay home with Liam while the other took Chloe. We let Chloe choose which of us she wanted to take her. I was selected for the prestigious honor. This was not the favored parent award I'd always dreamed of.

So, this morning Chloe and I woke early and got ready to be on our way. It's a sad state of affairs when a 10-year-old is dizzy with excitement for a three-hour drive to a doctor's appointment, only to then have to turn around and head home for another three hours. She was literally bouncing around the house because she was so desperate to go somewhere, *anywhere.*

While she was excited, I was nervous. The thought of going far from home, let alone a hospital, was definitely anxiety-provoking. While living in our self-imposed safety zone had its challenges, I certainly felt more protected than going out of state to a place with lots of (possibly sick) people.

The cleanliness of rest stops in New Jersey is questionable in the best of times, so I was not relishing bathroom breaks during a pandemic. But because of Chloe's bladder issues, making a three-hour trip without a bathroom break wasn't happening.

We were able to make it to Wilmington with only one restroom stop along the way. Surprisingly (gratefully), the rest stop was almost empty and very clean. Even better, we were the only ones in the ladies' room. Woohoo!

With little traffic along the way, we arrived at the hospital early and sat waiting in the car. When it was time to head into the belly of the beast, we donned our masks, entered the hospital lobby, and had our temperatures taken. Phew, we passed the temp test and were allowed to proceed. We were guided toward the Sunshine module. Along the way, we spotted a construction worker on a break, wandering the halls and wearing a hard hat. He was tapping his cell phone, mask comfortably resting on his chin. In a hospital. Nice. He protected his head but not his (or others') faces. Not happy. Point deducted.

We continued on our way to the Sunshine module and had to go to a reception desk to check in (another point deducted … here in NY, doctors ask you to check in from your car then head right into a patient room, hence no contact with a receptionist). I also had to hand her my credit card to cover my co-pay. You're making me pay to be here? Seems treasonous. To make matters worse, I had to sign the credit card receipt with a pen that the receptionist handed me. I don't have to sign a receipt at a grocery store. Why at a hospital? An unnecessary touch-point. Another point deducted. My anxiety increased.

Very quickly we were directed to Room 4. The doctor met us there. She examined, sanitized, tested, sanitized, made a call, and sanitized again. All that sanitizing was comforting. Chloe was sent twice to a restroom for a test, which was not comforting. At last the appointment was over, and we were sent home, sanitizing our way out of the hospital.

We got to the car and immediately shrunk down in the backseat to change our clothes. The dirties were banished to the trunk.

And, so, we began our return trip. Chloe was no longer giddy. She was remarkably patient and engaged in an audiobook, but the trip was long and tedious. Thank goodness for the fun snacks I brought for the occasion. We needed one bathroom stop along the way. This time, the rest stop was not so empty, not so clean. More anxiety. We were in and out as fast as we could manage.

Back in the car, in the relative safety of our auto bubble, we continued our trip. We made it home with minimal traffic angst. (Let's take a moment here to pause and marvel at a drive at 5:00

p.m. through the New York City area with little traffic. One glorious benefit I can attribute to COVID.)

When we got home, we each hopped in the shower and washed the day from our bodies, hopefully leaving any trace of a virus behind. I was so happy to be safe and sound in familiar quarters.

<u>COPAP Lessons of the Day</u>

- Some days aren't easy. There was a lot about today that I didn't love, but I'm grateful for a day spent with Chloe and the opportunity for an adventure outside our house.

- I'm grateful to healthcare workers who go into hospitals and doctor's offices every day. One day in a hospital, and I was a nervous wreck. I can only guess at how high the stress and anxiety must be among healthcare workers. I need to remember to thank them.

All masked up and ready to head into the hospital

Happy Camper

Liam was moody this morning. I've noticed a gloominess has come over him recently. This melancholy is very unusual for him, and it saddens me. I can't say I blame him. He's bored. He wants to be at camp. He wants to be with his friends. He's sick of spending time at home and in the yard with only his parents and sister. I get it.

Liam is the kind of kid who needs to be busy. Give him something, anything, to engage his brain and body and he's happy. Put him in a box, and he'll cheerfully make origami out of it.

If he's not occupied or has nothing to focus his attention on, it's grump city. He walks around, head hung, looking lost and forlorn. Keep him busy though, and he's a happy camper (sans camp, of course). So, it behooves me to ensure he has activities to do.

Today I came to the rescue. I found a garden stone project that's been hidden in the dark recesses of our basement for a year and a half. It involved making cement! It would be messy! There were detailed instructions! He was all-in. In another bit of good news, we had two sets of this project and the kids only did one before it started to rain. A second project in reserve for another day. Yes!

COPAP Lessons of the Day

- Kids need to play even if play is different from what we expected. I need to find ways to keep Liam engaged ALL THE TIME. He's taking some online classes this summer and playing outside, but he needs more. I'm now on a quest to determine what "more" looks like.

- My purpose of helping others reveals itself, and I will act on it, for both Liam's and my mental health.

Socializing

I can't believe it's July. I truly love summer. I wait all year for it. Summer brings an extra spring to my step. Sadly, I don't feel that usual joy this year. Too many emotions and too much uncertainty to deal with.

Tonight I did a fun summer activity, but it brought those difficult emotions with it. I attended an outdoor, socially-distant get-together with some friends.

It was a lovely evening—beautiful weather, nice friends, good conversation. As introverted as I am, I realized that even I have social needs. It was a real pleasure to be with people other than my husband and children (sorry, Dan, kids) to chat and laugh. I really enjoyed myself.

But the evening also had its challenges. I was constantly on guard ... checking my distancing from others, wondering if I should drink the beverage the host gave me, choosing to avoid foods that others brought, judging others for not wearing masks.

I wonder how the others were feeling. Were they comfortable? Were they judging me for being too cautious? They looked so calm. Were they truly relaxed or, like me, were they hiding their discomfort?

Life today is not simple or easy. It's hard to just relax and have fun.

COPAP Lessons of the Day

- Taking opportunities can be hard, but if I want to experience personal growth I can't avoid them.

- Adults need to take time to play too, almost as much as kids.

Butterscotch Morsels

Today I did something I hadn't done since the beginning of March. I went to the grocery store. Two stores, actually, because the first didn't have the darn butterscotch morsels Chloe needed for an online Harry Potter cooking class (butter beer and pumpkin pasties anyone?).

Today's experience of getting out of the house wasn't liberating. Rather, it left me with a strong desire not to go back to a grocery store for a long time to come. It was very uncomfortable. People wore masks, but many weren't distancing. I brought Liam and Chloe with me because I thought they needed an outing. I wouldn't bring them again. Too many people too close to them. Plus, they couldn't keep their hands away from their masks. It's not normal for them to have a swath of fabric across their faces. I get it. But the constant touching made me crazy. I couldn't get us out of those stores fast enough.

I'm ending my day with journaling and texting my friend Lori. Lori lives in Florida where COVID is spiking right now. I'm worried for her and her family. Her husband took a bad fall from a ladder last week and they're too scared of exposure to COVID to have him see a doctor. He's had two telemedicine appointments, but it's just not the same care as seeing a doctor in person. Then her oven broke, but they're too nervous to have a repairman come into their house to fix it. Her 16-year-old is struggling with the social isolation. Her 11-year-old is irritable. COVID summer is affecting us all. I tried to help and support her as best I could.

COPAP Lessons of the Day

- I sometimes take for granted the conveniences I get to enjoy. Today I'm taking time to be thankful for something as mundane as online groceries. (I'm not grateful for butterscotch morsels and butter beer, however. Bleh.)
- My purpose of helping doesn't mean I have to teach something. Helping can simply mean commiserating and being a (virtual) shoulder to cry on.

Sounds Horrible

This morning I took Liam and his friend for a bike ride. It was great to see the boys chatting and interacting, several feet apart, but still ...

We stopped at a small lake and they sat on rocks and chatted about school, friends, Harry Potter, whatever. These boys are pre-teens, and I see they need social interaction. It's such a hard balance to protect both their physical and mental health. It was nice to help them maintain both today.

When the friend's mom came to pick him up, she mentioned that their family was planning to rent an RV and go on a road trip for their summer vacation. She readily admitted that she is not an RV or camping kind of person, but their family had decided this was the safest way to vacation right now. So, they'll be packing up their three boys, a week's worth of food, and heading north in their monstrous RV.

I've been thinking about their vacation plan all day. Could our family manage a trip like that? "Hell no. Sounds horrible," Dan grumbled.

COPAP Lessons of the Day

- I often feel I have to take advantage of every opportunity that comes my way, but it's okay to pass on those that don't align with my (or my family's) desires or values. I just don't want to skip out on too many.

- It's okay to play at a distance (or whatever rules at the time dictate). Kids have fun playing with friends, even with restrictions.

Friendship, COVID style

Pandora's Box

Bright and early this morning we headed out to the ropes park we tried to visit last weekend. This time the weather was clear. No thunderstorms in the forecast.

Last week, I was very, very nervous. This time, I felt more comfortable. In the past week, I've been to a hospital, used public restrooms, socialized, and shopped in two grocery stores. After those activities, climbing ropes outdoors seemed downright tame. I realized that my actions, especially ones where I put myself out there and challenge my fears, really change my perspective.

So, off we went this morning, covered in our colorful masks and feeling fairly confident and comfortable.

We went to the outdoor sign-in area to register and buy protective gloves, required because of COVID. The gloves were not exactly what we were expecting, given they were supposed to protect against a highly contagious disease. They were fingerless, the kind where the top knuckle and fingertip aren't covered. The gloves seemed highly suspect, given they were meant to prevent a disease from spreading when you touch surfaces. It made no sense. Strike one against the ropes park. We had nothing else to wear, and at this point we really wanted to climb, so we hesitantly bought them and continued. Each time we finished a course and wanted a drink or snack, we ungloved and sanitized, especially our fingertips. Worrisome and annoying, but not enough to stop us.

The other concern of the day was getting harnessed. The staff members wore masks and so did we, but they still stood too close for comfort. When someone is fitting equipment around your shoulders and waist, where they can't rush because of safety, the degree of closeness is pretty intense. The proximity made sense, and we expected it, but it was still unnerving. I turned my head away (according to my family, in a very obvious fashion, like a belligerent child avoiding a scolding parent) to try to create some level of distance. Strike two. But we carried on.

From there, things got better. In the trees, families were distanced so we felt we could swing and climb safely without anyone breathing on us.

Strangely, my thoughts of safety were focused solely on the virus. There I was, 15, 20 feet off the ground (with my children, no less), hanging from a clip, and I was not worried about falling. Under ordinary circumstances the safety of the course would have been my concern, but it didn't even occur to me to worry about it today.

Once I felt COVID safe in the trees, the morning was fabulous. It was exciting and challenging, both mentally and physically. The children, who have done these types of courses more than we adults, gave us advice and guidance. They cheered me on and gave me confidence. For our last run of the morning, Dan and the kids went off on one course, and I went off on another. I felt good on my own.

We left, tired and spent, but very satisfied. So, here's the question. Do we go back despite the issues? I think so. We'll buy gloves that we feel comfortable in, so we'll avoid strike one. I don't think we can avoid strike two, the harnessing process. We either go and take a bit of a risk or stay home and give up a healthy activity. It's not an easy choice to make, but we've opened up a Pandora's box that will be hard to close again.

COPAP Lessons of the Day

- Sometimes, I have to decide if I'm okay with things I don't have control over. Accept or not? Today, I accepted, and I'm thrilled I did.
- Uninhibited play does wonders for mental health, for both kids and adults.

Climbing gear...check. Masks...check. Ready to climb!

Cleaning and Bashing

Today started with cleaning. Not an activity I relish, but one that desperately needed to happen. We normally have the luxury of a housekeeper who comes every other week. Since March though, we've given up this delightful indulgence. We have friends who've brought their housekeepers back into their homes, with the admission that maybe it was too soon, but they just couldn't give up the luxury any longer. We're being less indulgent, more cautious, and doing the work ourselves. Our health is more important than our dislike of scrubbing. Besides, it's good for the kids to appreciate the privilege they typically enjoy. And shouldn't everyone know how to scrub and vacuum? An opportunity to learn a new skill and feel grateful for our typical privileges. A win-win.

When the kids complain about cleaning, I don't give in as I sometimes do with their other grievances. I draw the line here. I refuse to do all the cleaning myself. I cheerfully offer to switch chores with them … I'll dust and they can clean the toilets. That quickly takes care of *that* discussion.

After lots of whining and protesting, the house sparkled. Well, not *sparkled* exactly, but it smelled really clean.

Once the work was done, the afternoon was more entertaining. Last week, Chloe took an online art class called "Let's Taco 'bout Piñatas." Holy guacamole, what a great name. Not surprisingly, she made a piñata. And, yes, it was in the shape of a taco. So weird, so fun. What's a piñata without a lot of candy and a bit of bashing? We filled it up, hung it from a tree, found a plastic bat, and whacked away until candy came pouring out. So gratifying.

COPAP Lessons of the Day

- Cleaning is an opportunity for my kids to learn life skills.
- I am grateful for the indulgences I get to enjoy. I don't want to become so jaded that I expect them.
- Work makes play so much more satisfying.

Love in the Time of Corona

We went to Grandma and Grandpa's for a barbeque. This meal had been in discussion for several weeks. Should we or shouldn't we go? Is it safe to eat food they've cooked, eat from platters they've handled, serve ourselves from spoons they've touched? We were hesitant, they were eager. Feeling a bit of pressure, we decided to give it a go. We set expectations about staying outside in the yard and distancing ourselves. We came up with a plan for Chloe to scurry inside to use their bathroom if needed.

We ended up being excited to go; we hadn't been to a barbeque all summer (except by ourselves, sadly, alone in our yard). We arrived wearing masks. Grandma, Grandpa, and my sister, Abby, all came outside wearing theirs. We distanced. After a few minutes, we discussed mask-wearing. We wore ours because we felt they would want it; they wore theirs for us. We all decided that as long as we distanced, the masks could go by the wayside. It's strange to have consensual conversations about masks of all things.

As time went on, they moseyed closer to us, and I became more uncomfortable. Grandpa put the food on our table for all to serve themselves. Abby came nearby to chat. Grandma stood right at the table to speak with us. She got closer, I backed away. What happened to our agreement to distance?

I was getting antsy and anxious. Finally I said something. I was uneasy telling my mom to step away from me, but I felt I should. I think she was a little shocked when I told her I was uncomfortable and to please back up, but she did it. As we got ready to go, we all agreed we should do it again, but I concurred only half-heartedly. As much as I want to see my family, I really wasn't comfortable. Is my anxiety making me unreasonably cautious, or is the wariness warranted? It's so hard to know. Life in this COVID world is not black and white.

The whole situation is unsettling. Health and family are at the top of my list of values. It's so hard to reconcile my feelings when family and health impact each other. I worry that prioritizing my family could compromise our health, while prioritizing health could compromise my relationship with my family. I don't think I've been faced with this dilemma before, and I don't know how to handle it.

I know my parents find both health and family important too, but, for them, family is paramount. They are okay with taking a bit of a risk to spend time together. Sigh. I'm struggling with this one.

COPAP Lesson of the Day

- I can't control my parents' values and priorities, only my own. We all need family and play, but sometimes it's hard to come to terms with these misaligned values. I want to find ways to play together that make everyone comfortable. I don't have a good solution yet.

MONTH TWO:
THE STRESSES AND REWARDS OF THE STRANGEST SUMMER EVER

The Mom Decree

My kids and I all enjoy cooking. It's gratifying to cook our own meals, be creative, and know what goes into our food. The kids have been exploring their interest this summer by taking a variety of online cooking and baking classes. From fajitas to profiteroles they are learning a number of cooking techniques and enjoying themselves in the process. And Dan and I are delighting in their output!

For several weeks, however, their cooking adventures have left me having to contend with the disaster area they leave in their culinary wake: a sink full of pots, a counter covered with ingredients, and a field of crumbs across the kitchen floor. I really didn't want or need this added chore.

So, after one of their "Cooking Boot Camp" sessions, I laid down new ground rules. You cook, you clean. I'd pitch in if there was a lot to do, but not do it all—or even most of it.

This Mom Decree has turned out to be a blessing. First (and best of all), I'm no longer doing all the cleaning. Woohoo! After today's class, I was delighted to see a (fairly) clean kitchen without my having lifted a finger.

Second, my children are learning practical skills for taking care of themselves when they grow up. I see Dan really uncomfortable in the kitchen. He never learned how to cook meals, clean pots, or even load a dishwasher properly. (I was shocked when I discovered this little gem while we were dating.) Our children will be better prepared. They definitely know how to load a dishwasher and then some.

COPAP Lessons of the Day

- I can control how much housework I do. The kids are old enough to contribute in a significant way.
- Play isn't only about fun. It's also about learning. What an opportunity when learning and fun come together.

Sacred Summer

 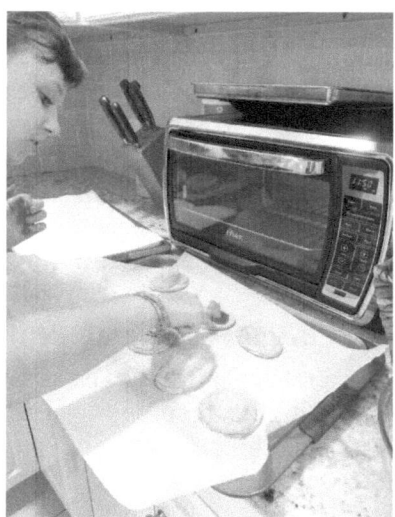

I don't have to cook tonight!

Mind-boggling Fun

Grandma and Grandpa gave us an escape room board game. As soon as they dropped it off, Liam ran to the dining room table to set it up and start playing. For the next hour and a half, both kids were engaged and fully immersed in the activity. It was so good to see. This is the kind of thing they need. Challenging, mind-boggling activities that require thinking and teamwork and, thank goodness, no screens. Seeing the wheels turning in Liam's mind was so satisfying for me and, I'm sure, equally satisfying for him.

COPAP Lesson of the Day

- Brainy play can be just as satisfying as on-screen play. The kids don't need screens (or me) to entertain them, but they do need help finding engaging, non-screen activities since the screens are so tempting and easy to access.

Busy Bodies

I've had a busy week and haven't had the energy to write at night. I see my self-care waning.

What am I so busy with? Work has picked up a little, so that's taking some time, but not enough to fill my days. What's really filling my time is the kids. I'm trying to keep them engaged and happy, which does not come without real commitment. I research virtual classes and programs, arrange outdoor play dates, and engage in the games and activities they want to play. It's a lot, but if I don't do it, their time will be spent playing on tablets, watching TV, and doing other mindless things. Not that there isn't room for those activities in their summer, but I don't want electronics overwhelming their days. I want them to use their brains doing creative, productive, thought-provoking activities and to move their bodies for exercise. And these endeavors require my time and energy.

The good news is, I think my commitment is paying off. I've found some amazing virtual classes and programs (some free!) for the kids. We're all getting exercise, riding our bikes, going for walks, and playing outside. And last night Chloe told me how much she's enjoying the things she's learning this summer, topics, she acknowledged, she wouldn't be learning if this were a regular summer.

She's had the opportunity to further a budding interest in writing. She's taking two writing classes to develop strategies for writing creative stories. One of the classes is free, sponsored by a museum in Rhode Island, and taught by a published author.

She is also pursuing her interest in space and planetary science. Recently, she watched the chief something-or-other at NASA talk about a massive telescope (it was so interesting, I listened in too!), staff at a New Jersey science museum discuss details about the moon, an astronaut discuss an upcoming SpaceX launch, and most impressive, watched amazing shots of planets, nebulae, stars, and other space things I can't name through telescopes located in South America. For $20, we signed her on to a website where she can access telescopes and take photos of her space discoveries. Before bedtime, she lies in her bed, enthralled, staring at these space objects on her tablet. Amazing.

Liam, meanwhile, is all about math, music, and coding. He's participating in an advanced math program with a gifted high school student who is volunteering his time to share his passion with other math-loving kids. Liam was annoyed when I first signed him up for the virtual, two-day-a-week class, but once the class started, he was all-in. The teacher gives problem sets for homework, which Liam does willingly, no complaints.

He can't do his piano lessons in person, but does them weekly via Skype with his regular teacher. He's advancing more than I would have expected, and the teacher gives no mercy. He is just as demanding and strict virtually as he is in person.

As for coding, Liam has learned html, Python, and Java, all from his desk at home. Tomorrow he starts a robotics entrepreneurship program.

Oh, and he's working on his bridge game. His Aunt Barbara, his grandpa (Papa), and Dan all play bridge, so the four of them play a regular (virtual) game three afternoons a week. Liam's brain is definitely engaged.

COPAP Lessons of the Day

- I can't control the limitations this summer has imposed, but, for damn sure I can—and will—make the best use of my children's' time.

- Yes, the kids are sad their sleep-away camp and climbing camp are cancelled. Yes, they miss hanging out with their friends. But this summer is helping them grow in ways they otherwise would not have had the opportunity to do. And that's not half bad, even if I'*m* worn out.

- There are so many opportunities to play. I just have to make the time to find what's out there.

Writing, Blogging, and Cooking. Oh my!

A rain storm was on the way, so before the deluge started Chloe and I headed out for a bike ride with a friend and her mom. There was a bit of complaining about leaving the house at 8:30 a.m., but it quickly subsided once the ride began. Though the morning was humid, it was cool and cloudy, making the weather very comfortable. We had a lovely ride around our favorite lake before stopping at a charming farmers market. I bought fresh bread and some leeks for next week's cooking class. Purchases on my back, we made our uphill return home. I made a deal with Chloe for next time: if she helps carry our purchases, I'll get her a chocolate croissant. She heartily agreed. A good deal for us both.

Once the rain began, we were stuck indoors. No worries though! Chloe worked on her story for the creative writing class she started this week. How satisfying to see her willingly and excitedly go into the fort she built in her room to do her writing. With each completed page, she came out to read me her creation. Just five pages in, it's amazingly clever. Even Liam told her it was really good. I never knew she had this interest and talent.

We also started a blog! Family and friends have been encouraging me to write a blog to share all the activities and projects our family has been engaged in. I've been considering it for a few weeks, but what cinched it was a friend who thought it would be a valuable learning opportunity for my kids. Bingo! That was the impetus I needed. An opportunity to help other families and keep my kids engaged, learning, and busy? I was all in. Another project to add to our summer repertoire.

The kids and I researched blogging, bought and registered a URL, and got to work. Liam started on the tech, Chloe wrote a blog post, and I started on my own post. By evening we had a basic website and two completed posts. In the next couple of days, we plan to launch it. We're all very excited to see where it goes.

The day also involved Chloe and Dan baking their dessert for our ongoing cooking competition. They made perfect lava cake in shiny, new, white ramekins. The chocolate oozed out just as it was supposed to. Now this is getting embarrassing. Dan has won both cooking competitions. I need revenge. We decided our next competition will be a gluten and dairy free meal. This will be my moment to shine. Bring it on.

COPAP Lesson of the Day

- Nothing earth-shattering today, just reinforcement of the importance of play and a reminder that when one door closes, another opens. These reminders keep me optimistic.

Oooh la la!

Sew Happy

It's 2:00 on a rainy Saturday afternoon.

Grandma and Grandpa stopped by earlier to have an outdoor lunch in our yard, but had to dash home when rain began falling.

Now that we're indoors, what to do?

I'm happy to say all is well and busy. Liam is sewing. On a sewing machine. No gender stereotypes here. Grandma taught both kids to sew last summer. She brought over her sewing machine today and now Liam is busy at work. He says he might start making masks.

Chloe is reviewing her creative writing story. It's now seven pages and, I'm told, complete, except for editing.

The best part is that both kids are sitting at the dining room table together, working and chatting. Liam has offered to be Chloe's editor. Chloe wants to help with sewing.

Meanwhile, I'm sitting nearby on the couch, watching, listening, and kvelling, as my Grandma used to say. It's so lovely when they want to help each other. I'm taking it all in and enjoying their sibling camaraderie.

COPAP Lessons of the Day

- I am grateful for moments of sibling love and support because goodness knows they won't last.
- We can support each other in our chosen forms of play. Who knows, we may even discover a new interest.

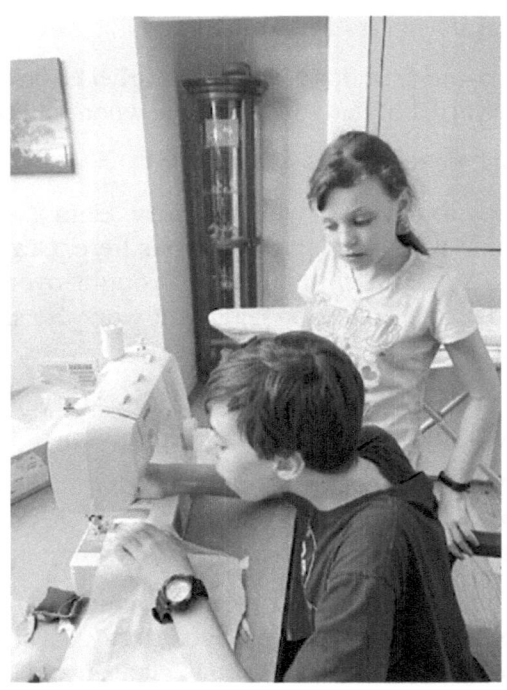

Such devoted siblings (for now)

Is a Hot Dog a Sandwich?

I'm supposed to be doing my research to prepare for a debate Chloe and I will be engaging in later this afternoon. We were discussing the concepts of Model Congress, Model U.N., and debate club at dinner the other night. Chloe was fascinated with the idea of debating and suggested our family try it. In the spirit of keeping busy and trying new things this summer, I figured, why not?

Now I know why not. I'm completely unmotivated to do my part.

Chloe and I will debate the question, "Should classroom pets be allowed in schools?" I will defend the "yes" position through a random drawing. Reluctantly, Chloe will defend the "no" position. She is already fully prepared. She conducted online research and wrote up her notes. Her diligence truly amazes me.

I, on the other hand, have done nothing to prepare. Chloe makes me feel humbled. She's also lighting a fire under my butt.

***

I finally prepared, and the debate went off beautifully. Chloe and I dressed up for the occasion (I don't remember the last time we did *that*) and used music stands as make-shift podiums. Chloe was fantastic. Following the guidelines we'd set, Dan and Liam selected me as the winner, but Chloe owned her position like a champ. If I didn't have close to 40 years on her, she would have taken me down. Her thoughts were organized and convincing, she was poised and confident. I'm not looking forward to her teenage years when she'll be able to make a strong case against everything I suggest.

Hmm, perhaps training kids to debate is not in a parent's best interest ....

Dan and Liam will debate next. Their debate question asks, "Is a hot dog a sandwich?" I can't wait to hear what their thoughtful research reveals.

COPAP Lesson of the Day

- I may not want to participate in my child's form of play, but it's so worth engaging for her development (and mine too!).

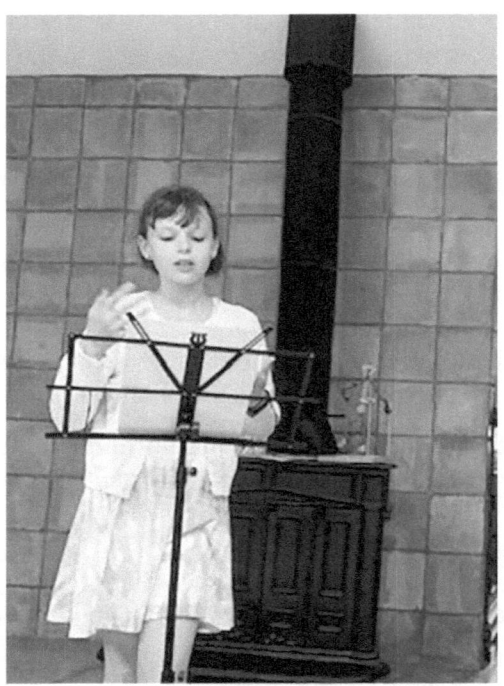

Debater extraordinaire

Physically Daunting

I really challenged myself today at the ropes park. I finished two intermediate courses and two advanced courses, and completely skipped over the beginner courses. Me! On advanced courses! Anyone who knows me well knows I'm a scaredy-cat. I'm in no way a daredevil or risk taker. It still boggles my mind that I felt motivated to try these courses in the first place, let alone go on advanced courses with elements that are 25 feet off the ground and require swinging, jumping, strength, agility, and other words that aren't usually attached to me. Perhaps there's a little embarrassment that my 10-year-old goes on these courses without fear, but there's more to it. I had this inner desire to challenge myself by learning something physically daunting.

It's interesting to contemplate the contrast between my ability to put aside fear when hanging from a wire but not when standing next to someone without a mask. Why the difference? Maybe because of a harness strapping me in safely and thousands of people who have climbed, unharmed, before me. With COVID there is no safety net, and very little history of success. The lack of security and knowledge is scary.

COPAP Lessons of the Day

- Becoming aware of my distress around COVID is a huge step toward gaining control over the fear.
- Not giving in to the fear of climbing is a lesson for so many challenges in my life. I can choose to sit back and watch, or take the opportunity to tell myself that I'm stronger than my dread and go all in.

Achy Brain and Armpits

Ouch. The glow from yesterday's climbing achievements is wearing off, and the aches are settling in. I'm sore in places I didn't know I had muscles. My armpits hurt.

We had a slow afternoon physically, if not intellectually. Dan, Liam, and Chloe love playing insanely hard board games. And by insane, I mean strategically so challenging many adults in my family won't play. (I count myself among these wimpy family members.) These games make Risk look like a day at the park. They make my brain hurt as much as my armpits. Why, oh, why can't my kids be entertained by normal games like Life and Clue?

I spent the afternoon watching in amazement as they played their Mage Knight game. It's so big and requires so many pieces it takes up half the dining room table. The other half is taken up by an even larger and more intimidating game called Rebellion. Each game takes days to complete. Good thing I have no dinner parties planned.

COPAP Lessons of the Day

- Having the guts to try something daunting can stretch me in equal parts emotionally and physically.

- I'm so grateful for Dan who has a knack for and an interest in strategic games because, goodness knows, I certainly don't. These games stretch them all in incredible ways.

Can't we just play Clue?

Risa Seelenfreund

Masked Man

Could this summer get any more inconvenient? Well, yes. Yes, it can.

Yesterday evening I came back from a bike ride wondering why I wasn't cooling down. I washed my face with cold water, changed my shirt, drank Gatorade, but I just couldn't cool my body. I checked the thermostat. Ah, it's not the start of menopause (thank goodness), it turns out our air-conditioner was broken.

If we wanted it working again (which, duh, we did), a repair person would have to come into our house. No one had entered our home since March 10. We weren't planning to start inviting guests in, let alone strangers. But no air-conditioning in July (with a heat wave on the way) called for special dispensation.

So, today, a mask-clad stranger entered our house. He was respectful, kept his face covered, kept his distance, but it was still uncomfortable. How do I know where he's been? How do I know if he wears a mask or social distances when off the job? I don't. I had to hope for the best and trust that the masks would do their job.

After he left, I sprayed disinfectant in the basement and den, where he had been, then wiped down door knobs and light switches he had touched. Was I going overboard? Maybe, maybe not. Again, I don't know him and his habits. I do know how careful we've been, and I don't want to jeopardize our commitment to staying healthy and safe. I can only control our actions, not his.

Unfortunately, this was not the end of the visits from our friendly, neighborhood masked man. Nor was it the end of our hot house. He calmly let us know a part was broken. An unusual part. A part that would take a WEEK to arrive. So, now we have to wait a week in a sauna (during the above-mentioned approaching heat wave), then have him back into the house to install the part.

Oh, and our washing machine is dying a slow death too. Since yesterday, it's up to the laundry gods whether it will turn on. We ordered a new one, which will be coming next week. This little delivery will require more workers in the house. Not just one person, but two, to carry and install the monstrous appliance. Oh goody.

COPAP Lesson of the Day

- Life has to carry on, things will break, and we've been lucky not to have had any serious issues so far. I wish our luck hadn't run out, but we will make it through. At least NY has low COVID counts now. We're much better off than my friend in Florida whose oven broke. How do you invite a stranger into your house with COVID running rampant and people in your area resisting masks? In comparison, we are very lucky.

Lemonade Out of Lemons

Hello lemonadeoutoflemons.org! Today our blog went live. Liam finished the tech, Chloe uploaded our first blog post, and I designed a fun, colorful background. Friends and family posted nice comments and subscribed. It was so satisfying to see the fruits of our labor show up online for the world to see.

We plan to keep this project going for as long as interest lasts. We've each written more posts, which we'll continue uploading.

At this challenging time, it's very rewarding to learn something new and create something meaningful and helpful. This endeavor feels good for my soul.

COPAP Lesson of the Day

- This is a learning and purposeful summer—not just for the kids, but for me too.

Our family website, www.lemonadeoutoflemons.org

Sacred Summer

Hot, Hot, Hot

I'm feelin' hot, just like Buster Poindexter crooned (and you too, Gloria Estefan).

We couldn't take the heat anymore and sent Dan out to buy a portable A/C unit. We set it up in our bedroom, and now all four of us are camped out in there. We dragged the kids' mattresses in and will spend the next week cozying up in our cramped bedroom. I'm trying so hard to feel grateful for what we have, but today I'm struggling.

COPAP Lesson of the Day

- Sometimes it's hard to be resilient. Even with strategies, tools and resources to use, it's not always easy to feel good during a difficult situation. I can accept that it's a tough day and know that things will get better.

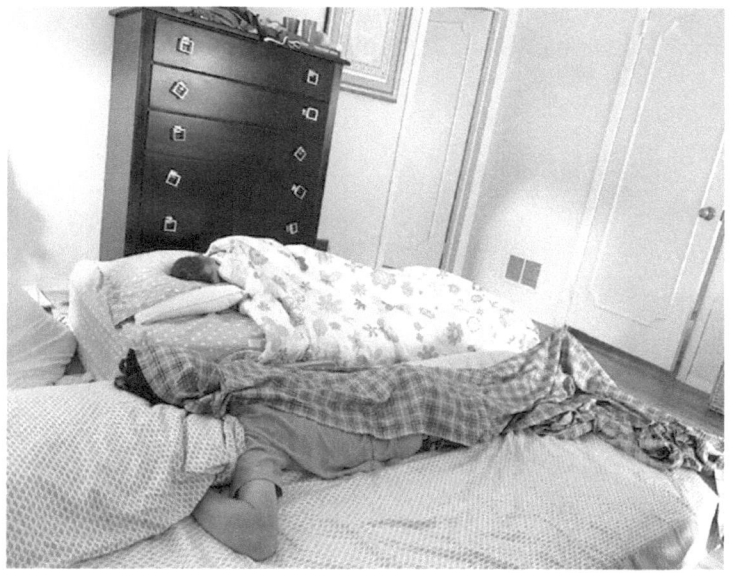

Cozying up in our bedroom

Virtual Anniversary

Today is Grandma and Grandpa's 61st wedding anniversary. Last year we had an amazing celebration week in New York City for their 60th. This year, things look quite a bit different.

Family can't fly in to celebrate. No way we could have a party. No desire to stay at a hotel. Or visit museums. Or, God forbid, kiss and hug each other.

So, we are celebrating their anniversary virtually this year. I snuck over early in the morning and hung balloons from their front stoop. Then we held a surprise family Zoom call with all the kids and grandchildren. Not ideal, but everyone participated, and we were all able to show we cared in the best way we could in this unusual year.

COPAP Lesson of the Day
- Take any opportunity to show up for the people you love, even if virtually (and stealthily).

Happy anniversary!

Subterranean Cave

My nephew, Jonah, is in quarantine. He returned six days ago from visiting his dad in Texas. Because Texas is on New York's quarantine list, he is required to quarantine himself for 14 days. He is living in Grandma and Grandpa's basement with a small refrigerator, TV, computer, and video games to keep himself busy. He seems oddly content with the situation. No one is bothering him to do anything. A happy teenager.

Eight days from now he'll emerge from his subterranean cave and rejoin the land of the living. Assuming, of course, he doesn't show COVID symptoms before then. Also assuming he chooses to emerge.

COPAP Lesson of the Day

- One person's misery is another's opportunity. Jonah is loving his quarantine? It's a complete mystery to me, but good for him.

Leap of Faith

Another Sunday, another morning at the ropes park. Today, we all challenged ourselves.

We were all doing an advanced course together, and I wrenched my arm on a swing element that I was terrified of last week. Ironically, I was much more comfortable going into it this time. Less scared, more confident, feeling like I got this. I swung assertively from the platform, holding on to a cargo net. As I approached the platform on the far end, I inadvertently swung backward and contorted my upper arm. Thankfully, Liam was on the platform and was able to grab me.

It shook my confidence. I felt good going into the swing element and frightened and disappointed afterward. I know I can't count on smooth sailing all the time (or any time, really), and that's frustrating. I wasn't prepared for a hiccup.

Two elements later, I almost got stuck in the middle when my foot slipped off a balancing peg. I frantically called, "Honey!!" as if Dan, who was in the middle of the next element, could come rescue me. He calmly suggested I step backward to the platform and start over since I couldn't proceed. I did, and took a few deep breaths. Now my confidence was really shaken. Nevertheless, I was determined not to give up. I tried the element again, this time without my foot slipping, but with the ropes swinging so wildly that I was almost in a split at one point. With loads of relief, I finally made it to the end of the element. Nervous, but with limbs intact, I continued.

The last element was upon me. Yay! Correction … ugh! It was the Leap of Faith. A free-fall jump that was all that lay between me and the ground. Oh how I wanted to be sitting at a picnic table with an ice pack on my arm. But I'd made it this far; I was going to make it. I was just terrified of the free fall. And my arm was killing me.

Without pausing, I stepped off the platform into the air and made it to the ground safely. Phew, I did it. Challenge accepted, fear managed, opportunity taken.

I was done for the day, but the rest of the family was not. They were going to challenge themselves with the expert course. Not I, thank you very much.

My family was amazing. They were 35 feet off the ground, swinging and climbing through the air. The course is meant more for adults than children, so the distance between planks, rings, wires, and other assorted paraphernalia was really tough for the kids. But they made it, hot, tired, and worn out. Another opportunity accepted and accomplished. I was so proud of them.

The rest of the day was spent indoors in our one air-conditioned room, recovering. Physically hurting but feeling great.

COPAP Lessons of the Day

- Sometimes I have to do things I don't like in order to succeed. In the end the difficult experience is worth it, but it can be hard living through it. It's tough to see the experience as an opportunity to learn and grow instead of a horrible, scary incident. I need to remember it's worth it!

- Play, play, play! It helps me feel good emotionally and spiritually (if not always physically).

Look! Up in the sky! It's a bird...it's a plane...nope, just Dan.

I've Got the Fever

It's 7:00 p.m. Not only are we exhausted and achy from today's climbing adventure, not only is the house—beyond our small, air-conditioned area of heaven—88 degrees inside, and not only do we have a washer that works only when it's in the mood, but now Chloe has a fever of 102.

In all likelihood, she has a urinary tract infection, an illness she's prone to, given her bladder issues. We jumped right into action when we realized she had a fever. Infections have happened so many times that we have a protocol to follow in an attempt to keep her out of the hospital, which, right now, is the priority.

We're pretty certain it's not COVID. She has no cough, congestion, sore throat, loss of smell or taste—the typical COVID symptoms. Just her usual fever and belly ache. Still, in the back of my mind the concern is there.

COPAP Lesson of the Day

- I can't control that Chloe gets infections, but I can gain some control of the situation by using what I've learned from the past to take action quickly, inform my decisions, and, ultimately, minimize the negative effects. What a powerful lesson during a difficult time.

The Elevator Shuffle

First thing this morning I dropped off Chloe's urine sample at a lab to verify her infection. This was my first visit to a medical building since early March. As I approached the elevator in the building, I hoped no one would enter with me. Mercifully, no one did. One person exited, and I carefully stepped to the side, then entered and stood on the opposite side from where she'd exited. So much coordination for something that used to be so mindless.

I entered the lab, which was practically empty. I've dropped off so many urine samples over the past two years that I can confirm it's typically uncomfortably crowded in there. But today the lab was shockingly quiet. I don't know if it's because they are limiting patients or because patients are choosing to delay lab work, but I didn't consider the reason for long before they took the sample out of my gloved hand and I was on my way back to the elevator, hoping, once again, for a solo ride. Happily, though two people exited (causing a bit of a shuffle as we all tried to distance ourselves from one another), no one entered with me.

I exited the building and removed my gloves. When I got to the car, I sanitized (with dreadful-smelling sanitizer since the pleasantly-scented varieties are sold out) before removing my mask. It's so strange that these steps have become routine.

COPAP Lesson of the Day

- My purpose is to help, especially my children. Even if it means putting myself in uncomfortable situations, I will not back down.

Shudder

It's confirmed. Chloe has a UTI. I'm not sure whether to feel relieved or upset. I'm certainly happy she doesn't have COVID, and the vile illness hasn't entered our sweltering fortress. But I'm not happy she has yet another UTI. With COVID, she would *probably* recover fine and have no long-term consequences. On the other hand, this UTI shows us that her bladder situation is not being well-controlled and may force us to make some difficult long-term decisions. Would COVID be better? Shudder. What an awful thought to consider.

COPAP Lessons of the Day

- Sometimes no option is good, and it's difficult to feel grateful. This thought won't help me build my resilience, but today is just hard. It's okay to struggle.

- I imagine it's hard for some frontline workers to feel strong and resilient day in and day out. I hope they realize it's okay to struggle under such difficult circumstances. I'm going to make a conscious effort to let them know how grateful I am for them and their hard work.

- Aha, something else to be grateful for: Chloe is not contagious. We can continue to huddle together in our one cozy room. Hmm…when I really think about it, there's an abundance to appreciate, even on difficult days.

Surface of the Sun

I spent today rotating between our cool, crowded bedroom and our hot (and I mean hot) office. It's a difficult trade-off. Either constant people and noise in a small space, or the quiet solitude of the sun's surface. Neither is a pleasant option.

Ordinarily, we'd escape a broken air-conditioner by leaving the house and seeing a movie or going to a mall or the library, even Costco ... some indoor, air-conditioned relief. But, movies, malls, and libraries are closed, and who wants to enter a large indoor space like a warehouse club? So, we stay home. And we deal.

We ate dinner in the kitchen, with windows open and ceiling fan on. The thermostat next to the kitchen read 90 degrees. Eating a meal when it's 90 degrees isn't fun when you're not at a pool with a margarita in hand. Ice cream for dessert? Now that made the situation a little better.

After dinner, we all headed back to the bedroom to cool down. I was ecstatic to watch the Broadway show *Hamilton* on television. The rest of the family decided to play a game. The three of them were on the bed with their sprawled-out game, and Mom, trying to hear and watch the Tony-winning show I've been waiting to see for years, was shoved into a corner. It was not the most relaxing or comfortable environment. I couldn't even straighten my legs. On the other hand, I finally got to enjoy *Hamilton*, and, in the immortal words of Mr. Hamilton himself, I was not throwing away my shot!

COPAP Lessons of the Day

- We can't control the heat in the house, but we can control what we do to make things a little more pleasant. We can only do what we can do. A cliché? Yes, but all too true.

- I recognize that a broken air-conditioner is simply a matter of inconvenience. It's what my family likes to call "a champagne problem." This designation doesn't mean it's not annoying and uncomfortable, but I'm trying to put things into perspective and be grateful for the important things like my family and my health (and finally getting to see *Hamilton*!).

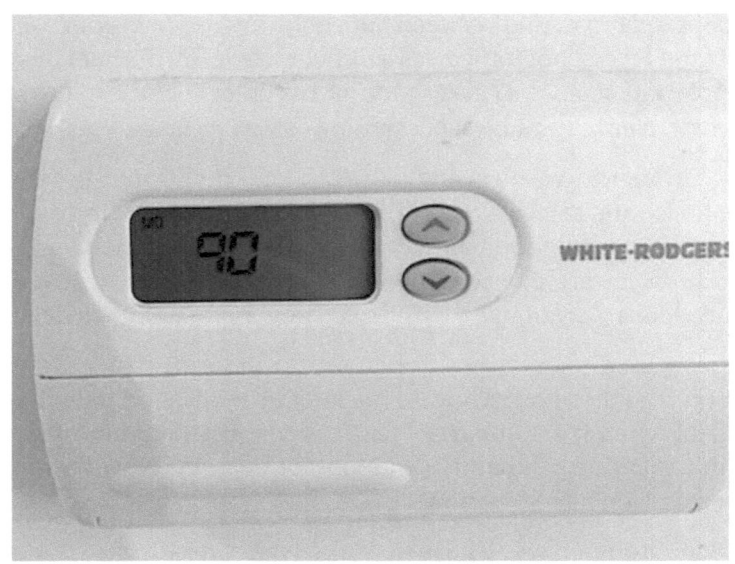
Look closely. It reads 90 degrees.

Barely any room for Mom!

Just Be

Day 8 without A/C. The stress of Chloe's UTI, compounded by the heat, is getting difficult to bear. I'm sick of being confined to one cool room in the house. We all are. We love each other dearly, but, good Lord, we all need some space. It's as though we're all sharing a hotel room with a fire just outside our door.

COPAP Lesson of the Day

- I realized today the parallel between dealing with the heat and dealing with Chloe's health issues: Until the A/C is fixed, the heat is here. I can't make it go away. What I can control is how I handle it. I can complain, be miserable, or just accept it and "be" with it—regardless of how uncomfortable it may be. The situation is similar to dealing with Chloe's health. I can't change that she has medical issues, but I can change how I deal with it. I can be angry, I can be miserable, I can complain that it's not fair, or I can accept the discomfort it causes. The more clearly I can think about and accept the situation, the better I can move forward with solutions.

A Good Night's Sleep

Hallelujah, the air conditioning has been fixed! At 5:30 p.m. the repair person came, like the Messiah entering our humble home.

An hour later, we felt cool air coming from the vent. It will take hours to bring the interior temperature down from 90 degrees to something more livable, but we're getting there, one degree at a time.

We will drag the kids' mattresses back into their rooms so we can all sleep in our rightful places. I'm thrilled to have the master bedroom back, but I must admit, I'm a little sad to see the kiddos go back to their rooms. It's been a fun (though crowded) distraction. Liam even said he'd like to do a family sleepover again. So, we will—but not anytime soon.

COPAP Lesson of the Day

- Look at that, family sleepovers: a new opportunity to play we hadn't planned for or expected.

Chillin' (literally)

One Large Mask

I had my first doctor's appointment since COVID struck. I was nervous to go, heart racing, sweaty palms, the works. But as Dan pointed out, I was going to the gynecologist so she'd be nowhere near my face.

I arrived at the medical building and was amazed at how empty the parking lot was. I usually have to drive around several times before finding a spot, hawk a patient who's leaving, or create my own spot. This time, I got the spot of my choice, in the shade, no less.

As requested by the doctor's office, I texted them from the car to let them know I'd arrived. A few minutes later, I received a text back, stating that they were ready for me. (Was I ready for them? Not really.) I walked into the building's vestibule and was pointed toward a nurse with a touchless thermometer and a bunch of masks. I was told to take a mask and put it on over my own.

I quickly realized that when it comes to masks (as with most other things in life) one size does not fit all. This mask was huge to the point where I had trouble seeing over it. Obviously, it was meant to be a comfortable fit for men, not petite women. Certainly, not this petite woman, whose brother makes fun of the narrowness of her face.

Clad in my double-mask, I headed up the stairs to my doctor's suite. I had so much trouble seeing that I had to look down at each step in front of me and watch where I was going so I wouldn't trip. Imagine breaking an arm or leg by trying to avoid COVID.

I chatted with the nurse while she checked my vitals. She told me that between March and sometime in May, Obstetrics/Gynecology was the only department in the building seeing patients. You can't exactly handle pregnancy as a condition whose treatment can be put off, and giving birth is not exactly an elective procedure to be delayed for a few extra months. So, they continued going into the office, as did the pregnant ladies, while the rest of the world stayed home.

While I was nervously dealing with the appointment, the doctor and nurse were acting totally normal. I guess when you've treated patients day in and day out during the peak of a pandemic, the current condition seemed mild. Once again, perspective reared its head. I remembered to thank them for their work.

When my appointment was done, I left the suite and cautiously made my way back down the stairs. Had I been willing to hold the handrail, it would have been less treacherous, but I was not about to touch anything. So, I walked down, carefully peering over my giant mask with each step.

At last, I made it to the exit, removed Mask # 1, and tossed it in the trash. I saved removal of Mask #2 until I was safely in my car.

I was thrilled I'd made it through the appointment, and, feeling giddy and brave, stopped at the grocery store.

Everyone inside the store wore a mask and most followed the directional arrows on the floor, which tried to regulate the flow of traffic. Despite the strict controls, I found shopping quite freeing. I made impulse purchases with abandon. I found everything I needed, and then some. I practically floated to self-checkout. Naturally, the last item I scanned had a glitch, and I had to summon help. I was so close. So much for avoiding checkout people. The worker, herself, wore a mask *and* face shield. I'm sure she didn't want to be near me either.

When I left, I felt so alive and uninhibited that I made one more stop at the butcher before heading home. Like the grocery store, everyone inside wore masks and most followed the directional signs, but employees and shoppers weren't so careful with distancing. I experienced both exhilaration and fear all tangled together, just as I'll probably continue to feel as summer rolls on.

COPAP Lessons of the Day

- I need to take small opportunities to get out and be free. Even running errands can be energizing and liberating after being cooped up.

- My lack of control over others' actions might be challenging, but, for my mental health, I need to get out of the house and into my community.

Boring

As we've done every Friday morning, today Chloe and I went for an early bike ride with her friend and her friend's mom. Then I did some work and some blog updating. Chloe and I went for a walk in the late afternoon, and then I made dinner. Nothing exciting. No illness, no crisis, no broken appliances, no drama. What a relief. I could use a boring day every once in a while.

COPAP Lesson of the Day

- I used to hate boring days. Now, at a time when life is stressful, the opportunity for a boring day is so welcome.

Our Friday morning social ride

Making Do

It was the best of times; it was the worst of times.

Let's start with the best part of today. Liam and I had a conversation about the summer and all that we've done so far. He said he was enjoying the summer and liked all the activities he's been doing. Woohoo! He also said he missed camp. He sheepishly admitted that he'd prefer going to sleep-away camp than being home, but then corrected himself to say that the best scenario would be camp for half the summer and "this" for half the summer. I'll take it! When I hear how unhappy and bored many kids are, I was thrilled to hear that he'd like to do "this" again next year, even for part of the summer. I was doing an internal happy dance. Talk about seeing opportunity in difficult situations and feeling grateful.

The worst part of the day? When the air conditioning broke AGAIN. Yes, again. After working for only three days. WHAAAAAHHH! And, of course, it's Sunday. No repair service until tomorrow.

COPAP Lesson of the Day

- Today was a metaphor for the summer and, really, the whole COVID experience since March. Highs and lows. Good times and bad. Thrills and disappointments. Opportunities and frustrations. Dealing with the unexpected. Making do until things get better. Take the opportunities where I can, be grateful for them, and just deal with the rest.

(Don't) Take Me Out to the Ballgame

Baseball season started four days ago. Today we heard that over a dozen players on the Florida Marlins tested positive for COVID. Oh, Derek Jeter, how can it be? The Marlins, as well as the Phillies, whom the Marlins played last night, have been instructed not to play until next week.

While I'm not overly concerned about the effect this issue will have on baseball season, I am very concerned about what it means from a broader perspective. If it took only four days for an outbreak to occur in baseball, what does this mean for schools when they're back in session? What does it mean for opening malls, movie theaters, and gyms?

A friend mentioned that some players were not following protocol off the field. They were interacting with others outside their bubble or ordering take-out food and exposing themselves to others. She said that perhaps these activities led to the outbreak.

Maybe they did, maybe they didn't. We don't know. What we do know is that the safety of the players and staff is only as reliable as the least careful individual on the team. The same applies for schools. Our family can be impeccably careful. Schools can have rigorous protocols in place. But … if schools open in the fall, and a family has not followed social distancing recommendations and requirements, a child can bring COVID into their school and cause an outbreak. If baseball can have an outbreak within four days, how long will it take for schools to have an outbreak? It's scary and unnerving. I feel my resilience being challenged.

COPAP Lesson of the Day

- I can't control other families' choices, only my own. It's hard to accept, but it's a reality I have to face. The best way to handle this discomfort is to focus on making good choices to keep my family safe. *That* I can control.

Busy Bees

I took Liam and a friend on a bike ride this morning. Of course, I heard complaints about leaving at the crack of dawn (it was 8:45, mind you), but it turned out to be a lovely ride. I was so pleased to see that Liam is getting stronger as we ride more and more this summer.

In the middle of the ride, we took a break at our favorite lake. The boys had a chance to sit and socialize. It was so nice to see their closeness despite the physical distance between them.

We returned by 10:00 a.m., in time for me to help Chloe get set up for a "MarsFest" online program about the launch of the new Mars Rover. Later, she took an optical illusions art class and a writing class. She also spent time playing catch outside with Dan and sharing with her aunt (by phone) a story she's writing.

At the same time, Liam got to work on all his summer projects ... making crossword puzzles, learning to play "Africa" on the piano, and playing bridge. He also made homemade guacamole and salsa to have with our salmon tacos for dinner.

Dan, meanwhile, was at his desk working by seven this morning. Business is picking up for him, and he's doing his damnedest to get more sales in before the end of the month. It's so good to see him busy and hear his stories about closing deals. It was hard not seeing him close much business for three months.

And me? I spent my day doing a little of everything ... bike riding, working, helping the kids, making dinner, attending Zoom calls. I'm finding it hard to focus for long on any one thing with the family being around me at all times. Truth be told though, while it's sometimes overwhelming, I do love the family swirling around.

COPAP Lessons of the Day

- Take a minute to step back and watch. Take in the opportunities and the play, and just smile for a moment.
- I'm grateful that my children are curious by nature and want to engage in activities. I know other parents aren't so lucky.

- I'm grateful that my work schedule is flexible. I feel for full-time working parents with an intense workload and bored children.

Feetloaf

Today began a week-long, virtual scavenger hunt sponsored by an organization called GISH. They offer hunts to raise money for a variety of causes and to have some good-hearted fun. This year's donations have focused on providing meals for children whose families have been impacted by COVID.

In the past, these hunts have been in-person. This year they are completely virtual. When you complete a task from the comfort of your home, physically away from your teammates, you take a picture or video of your completed work and upload it to a website.

I've put together a team of nine families for this hunt. Our goal to is to complete all 240 challenges within the next seven days. When we've done these hunts in the past, I've tried to press team members to do their best work and complete as many tasks as possible. I drove my own family (and myself) crazy insisting on high quality output and trying to get all the tasks done. But I realized that people have enough going on in their lives and that they are looking for fun, not pressure to have as much fun as humanly possible. Okay, I get that now. So, for this hunt, I'm being very laid back. Do as much or as little as you want. You want to do something simple? Fine. You want to go off-task a little. Okay with me. We're raising money, being creative, and keeping ourselves busy during a very challenging summer. What more could I ask?

So, what are some of the challenges we are being asked to complete? Let's see … making jewelry out of items in our junk drawer, creating a face mask for our car's grille, making a "feetloaf" dinner, asking our social media network to vote, creating an underwater campsite in a swimming pool, and on and on. The challenges are creative, socially aware, and downright hilarious. Perfect activity for this imperfect summer.

COPAP Lesson of the Day

- Let people play how they like. It's better for everyone, especially during difficult times.

Mmm....feetloaf
(Role of "Foot" played gracefully by Chloe)

School Angst

I'm starting to get unbearably stressed about school. We still have over a month to go before school starts, but the district is asking for our plans for the fall. Hybrid or remote schooling? I don't know. I see in the newspaper that an Indiana school district opened last week. (A quick aside: Schools opening in July? Who does that?) The district reported a COVID case on the very first day of school. Seriously? They couldn't even make it one full day? Well, that's comforting.

I read Facebook posts by people insisting children need to be back in school. I read posts that COVID won't end if we don't continue socially distancing. The most compelling piece I read recently was an essay by a dad who questioned why we are okay with sending our children to school but not okay with going back to our offices. And how we can accept sending children into classrooms but not accept attending face-to-face meetings with our colleagues. He asked 40 working adults he knew if they would attend a meeting with 12 people in a room. He said that every single one of them answered no. Some answered more strongly with "Absolutely not" and "Hell no." If we're not willing to take the risk, how can we put our babies in that position?

Dan and I feel fairly confident at this point that we will keep Liam and Chloe home. I think Liam will be fine. He works well independently, wants to work at his own (quick) pace, and is fine seeing a small cohort of friends one-on-one.

We're struggling with Chloe, however. She *desperately* wants to see her friends. She talks about it all the time. She doesn't want a structured, socially distant playdate with one friend in the backyard. She wants to hang out with her group of friends, have conversations that lead to organic giggles and games. I just don't know if we can give that to her. We promised we'd set up one-on-one outdoor playdates, but she is yearning for more. With her health history and the trauma it left us with, I don't know if we can accommodate her social needs. After all she's been through, she deserves fun and laughter, but how do we reconcile physical health and mental health? I know the value of mental health, and I don't minimize it. Yet, I think we need to prioritize physical health at the expense of her mental health, and it breaks my heart to even think about it.

COPAP Lesson of the Day

- Even decisions that are within my control, like choosing between hybrid and remote learning, aren't always easy to make, especially when neither one is an optimal solution. Dan and I will have to take what's in our control and make the best of a bad situation.

Lucky Ones

Today Tropical Storm Isais hit. Wow. Major rain and winds whipped through our county. Many, many households lost power and trees. We were among the lucky ones. We had lots of electrical flickers and some tree limbs down, but no power outage. Thank goodness. If we'd lost A/C one more time, I would have lost it. The summer has provided enough sweltering challenges. I can't take another. I'm feeling an abundance of gratitude.

COPAP Lesson of the Day

- Things will go wrong. When circumstances go my way, I can take a moment to relish my good fortune.

Risa Seelenfreund

Nervous Nelly

Much of our town and the neighboring towns still have no power 30 hours after the electricity went out. I feel incredibly thankful. I also feel terrible for those with no A/C (oh, how I can relate), food going bad in the fridge, phone batteries running out, and (possibly worst of all) kids with no TV or internet. I can hear the complaining ... "I can't go to camp, I can't see my friends, and now I can't even watch my favorite YouTube channel. I hate this summer!" I wouldn't blame them one bit.

So, while this morning I was feeling incredibly happy about our good fortune, I was also a Nervous Nelly because I had a dentist appointment. I hate going to the dentist under the best of circumstances. With COVID, I avoid going into enclosed places as much as possible, I wear a mask religiously when I have to go anywhere indoors, and I have seen only one doctor in the past six months, and she came nowhere near my head. Today, not only was I going to see another doctor, but one who would literally be in my face. While I wasn't wearing a mask. And to top it off, I wasn't sure what the drive to the dentist's office would be like, given the number of downed trees. STRESS!

Off I went on my tense journey that usually takes eight quick minutes. The drive was truly shocking. The streets looked like a war zone: power lines down, trees lying across roads, limbs strewn across lawns, police tape everywhere. I had to turn the car around a minimum of eight times because so many roads were closed.

Forty-five minutes later (and half an hour late), I finally arrived at my dentist's office. I wasn't even in the chair yet and I was already stressed. Not an auspicious start to the appointment.

As soon as I walked in, the overwhelming smell of cleanliness, sterile and satisfying, put me a bit at ease. I was greeted by a young woman who very graciously excused my tardiness and then proceeded to point me toward a bottle of hand sanitizer and latex gloves. She took my temperature and shared some safety information from a clipboard. Sanitizing, fever-checking, and information-sharing completed, she escorted me to a patient room. On the way, I remembered to thank her for her service.

There I sat with mask and gloves on, trying not to touch anything and making an exceedingly difficult effort to look casual. The hygienist walked in, covered in mask, face shield, and gloves—just as I was hoping. I removed my mask, and she got to work. She began cleaning my teeth, and, much to my surprise, managed to keep a good 10-12 inches from my face. She worked quickly, which I very much appreciated. I actually felt quite safe, with her mask and shield coming between my mouth and hers.

Finally, the dentist came in and took a look inside my mouth. He, too, wore a mask and shield and didn't linger in my face. So far so good.

Then things went a little south.

As I was speaking with the dentist, the hygienist walked in with her mask hanging around her chin. She was two to three feet from me, neither of us in a mask. I was annoyed and anxious, the common refrain of "When you cannot maintain six feet of distance from others wear a mask" running through my head. How can a professional who works in a dentist's office forget to pull her mask up when entering a patient room? I gestured to her to indicate that her mask was down, and she put it in place. I started questioning the wisdom of going to the dentist.

Things continued moving down south. The dentist told me that I should get a crown put on one of my teeth. Oh, and the crown may not work, and, if it doesn't work, I'll need a root canal. Ugh. In addition to the angst created by the thought of a possible root canal, I felt anxious over the thought of at least one more dentist appointment in the very near future to get the crown put on. I was hoping not to come back for a good, long while. Oh goodie, this day was getting better and better, and it was only 9:30.

My return trip home, which again should have taken me eight minutes, took 35. At least I shaved 10 minutes off the outbound trip.

Once I got home to our safe bubble, I felt instantly calmer. Oh, the comforts of a cozy womb.

COPAP Lesson of the Day

- Even if I'm hesitant and uneasy, I can take action to control an uncomfortable situation. I could have sat in the dentist chair seething, but instead I calmly let the hygienist know of the mask issue and was able to resolve it quickly.

Baking Blitz

I walked into the kitchen today, and both kids were busy, each one participating in a different baking class. It was comical. Chloe was at the kitchen table making snickerdoodles while Liam was at the counter making "monkey bread." Each was following along on a different tablet. The number of bowls, pans, crumbs, and ingredients was crazy. I knew the cleaning would be monumental. But, at that moment, I didn't care. I was just delighted to see my crew happy and busy.

COPAP Lesson of the Day

- Enjoy the play while it lasts. The crumbs can wait. Don't let the thought of the annoying stuff ruin the moment.

RIP Raindrop

This evening we took a family outing to Petco. This little trip was fairly significant, considering we haven't taken a family outing anywhere in the past six months. Why Petco of all places? Well, Chloe is desperate for a pet. With the difficulty she has been having with the likelihood of not going back to school in the fall, we thought we could bring some joy and excitement into her life with a furry friend. Even she has said that a new pet would make being home from school more tolerable.

Unfortunately, pets present some challenges for our family. We can't get a dog because Liam is allergic. We can't get a cat because Dan is allergic. We tried a fish. He was exceedingly dull until he died and we had to flush away his tiny carcass.

RIP Raindrop.

So, we have been exploring less obvious pet options. Our current pet of choice is a guinea pig. We've been researching these little cuties online. They seem cuddly and friendly, not too big and not too smelly. (Although, apparently, they are little poop machines.) We decided we needed to see and hold a guinea pig in person, see how we feel with a real, live one in our arms. Thus, today's monumental trip to Petco.

After our visit (the store was, thankfully, mostly empty of humans), we all agreed we liked guinea pigs and would be happy adding them to our family. (Note that we have to get more than one guinea pig. Evidently, they are social animals and prefer having a companion. How can we have one lonely piggie?)

One big hurdle remains, however ... allergies. With a cornucopia of allergies in our household, we run the risk of one of us being allergic to either guinea pigs or the mold in the hay they eat. Rather than face the possible trauma of having to return guinea pigs after bringing them into our home, we have decided to be proactive and all get tested first.

One of us had better not be allergic. I can't handle a scaly substitute pet.

COPAP Lesson of the Day

- Don't wait for a situation to fall out of my control. I can take proactive steps like getting allergy tested to maintain control before a ten-year-old girl is distraught that a pet has to be taken from her.

Play Date

Chloe had a friend over for an outdoor, socially-distant play date. It was both lovely and sad to see. The good part was that they had a fun time together chit chatting, crafting, and biking. They both eagerly said they want to do it again. Success! The sad part was they wore masks the whole time and stayed six feet apart from each other. It was heartbreaking. That they enjoyed this type of play date so much was equally as sad. At least *they* were happy.

COPAP Lessons of the Day

- Take any opportunity for joy and entertainment, even if unconventional.
- Play when, where, and how you can.

So happy to have a play date

Family Fun

I love that my extended family wants to play, even remotely.

Today Papa decided to start a family caption contest. He emailed us all a quirky photo and asked everyone to submit their funniest caption. From age 10 to 82, we all sent each other our humorous entries. There's no tangible prize, but he created an opportunity for us all to be in touch and bring a smile to each other's faces. Prize enough.

We also held a virtual family game night. This event was all Liam. He decided we should play bingo. He found a free, online bingo app, sent everyone instructions, and was our stellar bingo caller ("B4 and after!"). Simple and fun. Just to see everyone's faces on Zoom and hold side conversations in between games was a great way to spend an evening. I must say, I'm disappointed that Dan won two games and I won zero, but I'll get him next time.

COPAP Lesson of the Day

- I don't think we would have taken the time to do these silly activities any other time, but why not? They're fun and engaging. No reason not to continue with these enjoyable opportunities to play together even when things are back to normal.

Treasure Chest of Electricity

I have reached my breaking point. I've been trying to focus on the positive, the family time, the unusual adventures, but today I reached my limit. I'm done. I can't take any more challenges.

Last night at 9:35, we lost power. Out of nowhere, everything went dark. No storm, no loud pop, nothing. Just blackness. We thought we'd dodged a bullet by not losing power during the storm a few days ago, but nope. The bullet found us.

Enough already. Concern about COVID, no camp, no work, broken A/C, Chloe's UTI, worries about school, and now no power. I can't take this summer any more. Let it end. Typically, this thought is abhorrent to me. I never, ever want summer to end. I go into a little funk after Labor Day because summer is over. Summer 2020, however, has beaten me down. I'm done. I'm ready for it to be over.

I completely lost it this morning. I hid in the bedroom, curled up on the bed, and cried. I knew I couldn't solve anything from my pillow, but I needed the space to let it out. I'd held it together until then, but I couldn't hold it in any longer. The cry was good, cathartic.

After allowing myself some time, I headed downstairs and found Dan and the kids emptying out the fridge and freezer into grocery bags.

When all was packed up and ready to go, we headed out to deliver our packages to our parents. To be more accurate, we delivered our packages to their doorsteps, so *they* could bring them in. Not to be rude or anything, but we didn't want to enter their houses. We haven't been inside their houses since early March, and we weren't going to start now.

Once we dropped off our groceries and chatted in our parents' driveways, we ordered a take-out lunch from our favorite diner. We had no desire to head home to our sweat lodge, so we took our lunch to the park and ate in the shade of a large tree. As we ate, we looked out onto Long Island Sound and the boats floating in the water. It was truly lovely. It was serene and peaceful. I breathed deeply and took in the view. As awful as the morning was, the fresh air of the afternoon cleared my head. The beauty and calm in that park helped me have some perspective. The next few days would indeed be annoying and difficult, but there was something bigger and more beautiful to appreciate than to focus on my discomfort.

After lunch, we walked around the park and stopped at a small playground. By the time we returned to the car, I was in a much healthier frame of mind. We returned to the same hot(ter) house, but I was feeling considerably different.

At home, we sat quietly, trying not to expend any unnecessary energy. I read while Dan and the kids played a game. It was calm and tranquil.

Out of nowhere, Dan remembered that Papa had an old generator. Why it took all day to recall this critical bit of info remains a mystery, but Dan grabbed Liam and headed back out to Papa's house to pick up this treasure chest of electricity.

They returned with generator in hand!

Because we no longer had food in the fridge or freezer that needed to be kept cool, we decided to focus on using this little box of joy to keep us comfortable. We hauled the portable A/C unit (from our broken air-conditioner days of two weeks ago) back up to our bedroom and planned for another family sleepover. Chloe and I sent down wires from the bedroom window, and the guys powered up the generator. We crossed our fingers and toes and turned on the portable unit. Woohoo! It turned on, and cool air started pouring out. We shouted with genuine glee.

And, then, the gem started smoking. Thick, white smoke that traveled across our yard. As a precaution, Dan turned it off. He checked the unit, googled some stuff, and turned it on again. The thick smoke came back with a vengeance, and we knew it wasn't safe. We were crestfallen. No power for us. I (not very successfully) tried to stay positive and put things into perspective.

At 6:45 we sat down at the kitchen table for an elegant dinner of peanut butter and jelly sandwiches. By now, the effects of the serene water and beautiful park had worn off. My petty problems were looming larger. I was hot, the shadows in the house were getting longer, and I was eating PB&J on stale, gluten-free bread on a Saturday night.

We were all starting to feel a little miserable. After living through the broken air-conditioner for more than a week so recently, we had had it. We were done with living in a sauna.

At 7:30, Dan called Papa and said we were coming over. Let's pause a moment to consider the significance of this decision. We had barely left our house since March. We hadn't entered anyone else's house, even our parents', since March. Now, we felt desperate enough to accept an invitation to stay with someone, COVID be damned.

As uncomfortable as we felt about going into someone else's home, at this point we were too uncomfortable to stay in our own. We were physically hot and emotionally spent. So we quickly packed up a few things and headed over to Papa's.

I'm in bed, and it feels like heaven. We are cool and comfortable, physically, if not emotionally.

COPAP Lesson of the Day

- I'm taking stock of my resilience. I could not control the heat or the lack of A/C, but I could control my response. Although I struggled with it, I did find solace for a bit in the park. I made the decision with Dan that we needed to get out of the house for the night. We're making decisions and moving forward based on what we can control, and that brings a little bit of comfort.

Breathe and take in the view. Ahh.

On Vacation

Today we joked that we're taking our summer vacation at Papa's house in Rye, NY, 20 minutes from home.

The joke was funny but also sad. We've chosen not to go away this summer. We weren't going to get on an airplane. We had no desire to stay at a hotel, we weren't going to eat in restaurants, and individual vacation homes were very hard to come by. Thus, the joke about vacationing at Papa's house in Rye was all-too-true.

We had a very good day at Chez Papa. Papa was up early and made breakfast. We then headed out for our usual weekend trip to the ropes park. I think it was my best ropes course experience yet. My arm was finally feeling healthy, so after my stint on the disabled list, I was ready to try an advanced course again. To be sure, I was very nervous. It was hard last time, plus I got hurt. I felt it would not be easy to get back on again, but I was determined to do it.

When we arrived, we started on an intermediate course. All went smoothly and easily. I knew I was ready for the next step. Dan thought I should try an advanced course I hadn't done before. I wasn't so sure, but I agreed.

I climbed up nervously to the start of the course. I began slowly and cautiously. It was a challenge. Dan and the kids encouraged me, which was a tremendous help. I started to get more comfortable. My confidence grew, and I felt good. Really good. I stopped—fully stopped—to look around, to take it all in. I felt energized. I was about 25 feet off the ground, hanging by a wire, and balancing my way along swinging obstacles. I was doing it, and I was feeling great. Before I knew it, I was at the last element, the Leap of Faith. Why does it always have to end with the Leap of Faith? Before the panic had time to take hold, I jumped. I hated it, but I did it. When I landed on terra firma, I was truly happy and proud of myself. I lifted my arms in triumph. My Rocky moment. I was thrilled.

We returned to Papa's house for a relaxing afternoon. While Dan and I napped (what a luxury!), the kids hung out and played games with Papa. I don't know who had a better time ... the kids or Papa. It was such a treat for all of them to spend so much time together. The last time they spent a considerable amount of time together was last November, before Papa left for Florida for the winter. Never would we have expected that he'd return to NY in the middle of a pandemic.

In the evening, Dan and the kids went upstairs to watch television. Papa and I stayed in the kitchen and chatted. We had a real conversation about politics, society, and race. These discussions happen so infrequently. We usually talk about the kids or inconsequential, silly topics that have no real meaning. This conversation was full of substance and significance. It was insightful and thought-provoking. I felt fulfilled and challenged. It was a perfect way to end an unexpectedly gratifying and happy day. Just like a real vacation, and only 20 minutes away in Rye.

COPAP Lesson of the Day

- I was all over building resilience today. If I just look, I can find plenty of opportunities to learn and grow:
    - Focusing on what I can control by challenging myself at the ropes course? Check.
    - Turning fear into opportunity? Check.
    - Living my purpose by helping Papa think about things in a new way? Check.
    - Feeling infinitely grateful for my family? Check.
    - Playing? Definitely.

Renegade Blueberries

Let there be light! Last night at 9:00 we were blessed with electricity. Chloe was already in bed and Liam was in the shower, so we decided to remain at Papa's for the night and head home this morning.

Dan and I headed out bright and early. Liam and Chloe were sad to leave and really had no reason to rush home, so to their delight (and Papa's) we left the three of them until later in the day.

Dan and I got home, cranked up the A/C, unpacked, and did some work. Later I took the opportunity to clean the empty refrigerator. Yikes, it needed it. You don't realize how much it needs a cleaning until it's empty, with nothing to cover up the sticky spills and renegade blueberries.

What a great metaphor for life: Only when we lay ourselves bare are we able to see our flaws and clean ourselves up.

COPAP Lesson of the Day

- At dinner tonight, we spoke about resilience. I reviewed my COPAP model with the family, and I realized it can work for kids. We discussed that our weekend with Papa was a perfect demonstration of the strategies .... We couldn't control the power outage, but we were able to control our attitude and actions in dealing with it. We had the wonderful opportunity to stay with Papa for the weekend. Our purpose right now is keeping ourselves and others healthy. (Not our reason for being on this earth, but this worked well enough for the kids.) We were grateful for family to stay with. We had so much fun playing with Papa. The kids understood and absorbed the concepts. The discussion worked better than I'd expected. I will continue to remind the children of these tools to help them build their own resilience during this complicated summer.

MONTH THREE: FINDING PEACE

What We Can Hold Onto

School STRESS.

More and more school districts around the country have started their school year. We see images on television of innovative social distancing measures taken in elementary school classrooms while we also view overcrowded high school hallways. We watch children entering schools and exiting buses, some in masks, some not. We hear reports that the count of children testing positive for COVID19 is increasing. It's all very disturbing.

Our children start school in a month. We'll watch to see what happens with children in Georgia, Texas, and other states before we enter our New York coal mine. Those children are the canaries we're keeping an eye on to see what lies in store for us.

In preparation for school, today we had a telemedicine call (a new phenomenon we're still getting used to) with one of Chloe's doctors. This particular doctor heads the infectious disease department at our regional children's hospital. If we wanted to hear the down and dirty on the current COVID situation, especially for children, she is the doctor to speak to.

She gave us somewhat reassuring news that she felt Chloe could go to school without any additional risk from her past medical issues. Okay, this is good news. But the doctor couldn't be sure. Okay, not-so-good news. What I took away from the call more than anything else was how much is still unknown about this virus. Doctors don't know why some perfectly healthy people get extremely sick. They don't know why it affects some people's hearts. They don't know why so many children are asymptomatic. They don't know exactly how it spreads. This ambiguity is unsettling. So, we could send Chloe to school two days a week and she probably wouldn't have a severe case of COVID if she caught it, but we don't really know. We also don't know if anyone else in the family could catch it and have a severe case.

The uncertainty and lack of control is causing me an incredible amount of anxiety. I can send Chloe to school and her emotional health will thrive. But her—and the rest of the family's—physical health could suffer. Or, for her physical health and ours, I can keep her home in our bubble and make her miserable. I'm struggling to reconcile physical health and mental health. I've always prioritized physical health, but this girl has been through so much. I don't know how much more I can sacrifice her mental health and keep her whole.

****

News flash. Later in the day we got word that our school district has made a change. The school year will open in September entirely virtually. There will be no in-person classes for the month of September. We don't know what will happen come October, but this is the plan for the beginning of the school year.

Dan thinks it's "fantastic." Chloe is gloomy. Liam is thrilled. I'm uncertain. I've spent most of the day trying to get comfortable with the idea of sending Chloe to school. And now this change. I suppose I'm relieved for our physical health, but this turn of events only delays our decision for a few weeks.

I get it, though; the virus is in charge here, not the school superintendent, not the government, not me. We need to bow to its whims, no matter how difficult, so we can all be safe. Focus on the things we can control, right?

COPAP Lesson of the Day

- Having control means not being at the mercy of my circumstances. I know I need to focus on what I can control, not the things taken out of my control, like COVID and the school district's decisions. Dan and I will decide the steps to take to keep the children healthy during the school year. That much we can hold onto.

Micro Learning

I've been busy and not in the mood to write recently.

Busy with what? I'm not sure. Work is somewhat slow, so I can't attribute excessive busy-ness to that. I'm not taking the kids anywhere, so I can't blame them for Mom's taxi service. I'm just busy with daily stuff ... laundry, cooking, helping clean up after the kids' baking classes, going to doctor's appointments, finding interesting online classes for the kids. I don't know ... the days just go by, and I'm not sure where they're going. It's making me feel sad. I'm not feeling motivated to get up and get going each day.

Writing is making me realize that I need to work on my resilience. It is definitely floundering. In particular, I need to focus more on my purpose to help and teach. While I'm definitely helping my children keep busy by finding them interesting and educational activities, I'm not doing enough teaching and training of adults. I'm realizing that I sorely miss it. In the spring and early summer, I regularly created "micro learning episodes"—short training videos—for my clients. I enjoyed it and felt as if I were providing some value during a difficult time. But I've let the videos slip recently because they take a good amount of time. Plus, I need to enlist Liam's help with editing.

I've lost my motivation, and the work just doesn't seem worth it.

COPAP Lessons of the Day

- It's time to record more micro learning episodes. Despite the time and effort involved in creating them, they bring me joy. They link me to my purpose. They make me feel as if in my own small way, I'm doing something to help. If I can't facilitate classes in person, and no one needs workshops developed right now, I can still do *something*. And, maybe, just maybe, they will bring in more business. At the very least, they will help others and make me happy.

- While it's hard dealing with the slow-down of my business, I'm lucky to have time to cook, clean, and find activities for my children. Many, many parents are struggling with working full-time while having to keep their children occupied and take care of their home. Then there are essential workers who have to leave the safety and comfort of their homes each day to go to work. I feel grateful for my situation.

Mystery Box

We tried a new cooking competition today: Mystery Box! Chloe and Dan secretly selected six ingredients for Liam and me to use. We had ninety minutes to look at the ingredients, research recipes, and cook our best dishes. Chloe and Dan then judged the fabulous feast each of us created. Ooooh ... exciting!

Our stringent judges selected cod (again?), oats, almonds, sweet potatoes, apples, and sundried tomato almond flour crackers. How to concoct them all into a delicious meal?

Liam and I scrambled around the kitchen trying to stay out of each other's way. We had a great time competing. The star of Liam's dish was his fish ... coated in mustard, dipped in crushed almonds and crackers, then baked. My star was a sweet potato and apple puree topped with roasted almonds.

Unfortunately for me, Liam eked out a win. If you're keeping score, I have yet to win a cooking challenge. I like to think that my family is defeating me because I've taught them everything they know about cooking. Yes, let's go with that.

COPAP Lessons of the Day

- I'm humbled for sure but also proud of my family for taking the opportunity to put their best foot forward and beat me.

- Liam told me how much he enjoyed the competition. On the cusp of thirteen, he could be ignoring us. I'm thrilled he still wants to play with us instead. As long as he wants to engage, I will provide opportunities.

Crowning Moment

This morning I went back to the dentist to have a crown put on. Sadly, it didn't make me feel like a princess.

It took many deep breaths and muscle relaxation exercises to get me through the appointment. It was as scary as going on an advanced course at the ropes course. I knew if I could manage the Leap of Faith, I could also manage a dental appointment.

My tooth is very uncomfortable now, and I have to go back again in two weeks for the permanent crown. At least there won't be any drilling (or a Leap of Faith) at that appointment.

COPAP Lesson of the Day

- I can gain strength by recalling past difficult experiences I've conquered. Remembering how I've succeeded in the past can help me gain control of a daunting situation.

Me and My Girl

Chloe and I went for a beautiful bike ride early this morning. It had just rained, so there was some moisture in the air, but the air was cool. Because it was still wet, not many people were out. The neighborhood was peaceful and quiet.

I'm so enjoying these morning rides, especially when my girl comes with me. It's a calm, bonding time for us. It helps me get to know her better. It's especially nice when the air is fine, and we return home without turning into wilty, melty messes.

COPAP Lesson of the Day

- Play by myself is healthy and relaxing. Play with someone else takes it to a whole new level of enjoyment.

Cycling partner

Together Yet Apart

Today the kids and I went peach picking. We do our annual trip to the apple orchard every fall, but this was our first foray into the world of peaches.

Pro tip: Fall apple picking is much more comfortable than summer peach picking. The temps are MUCH cooler and humidity much less. Peach picking in August is a sweatfest.

Still, we had a ball. Our activities have been so limited that crossing the bridge into New Jersey made for an exciting adventure.

Even better, we made plans to meet Liam's friend and his mom at the orchard. How nice to find an activity that we could all enjoy together—yet apart—outdoors.

When we got home, we made peach applesauce and a peach crisp. An extremely good day!

COPAP Lessons of the Day

- Opportunities may not be perfect, but we can still enjoy them. It's not worth waiting for perfection.
- Even uncomfortable play is worth it!

Looking peachy!

Watershed

My sister, Abby, and her son, Jonah, came over today. Liam, Chloe, and Jonah had a fun time with water balloons and the Slip 'N Slide. Sadly, the slide got a big hole. We've all acquired some wounds this summer.

It was a hot, still day. Our yard is shady and usually has a nice breeze, but not today. At one point, Abby asked gently if we could possibly move indoors because she was getting overheated. It was a watershed moment. Do we let them inside the house and open up the door to other family members? We had been contemplating having family come into our house in recent days, and now was the moment for a decision.

We made up our minds to welcome them in. I know Abby and Jonah have been very careful and have barely gone out of their house, so we figured the risk was low while the desire to spend more time with them was high. It was stressful for us though, and a big step forward.

And, then, we got even braver!

Chloe has been feeling blue. She misses her friends and desperately wants to go back to in-person school just like so many other children. Plus, she misses the way summer "should" be ... going to camp, hanging out with friends, having sleepovers. She complains that it's not fair to spend an entire summer without splashing in a pool.

So, yesterday, I mentioned to Dan how sad she's been, and we decided we need to do something to support her mental health. I suggested we look into joining a local pool for the rest of the summer (an uncrowded one, of course). Dan surprised me by suggesting we go away instead.

Wow, I was not expecting that. I wasn't sure. Should we?

We decided to dip our toes in to the possibility of a vacation by researching if any rental houses with a private pool were even available. Turns out, there wasn't much availability for a small house for four people within driving distance. Oh well.

But then ... today we told Abby that we were considering going away for a week, and she said she and Jonah had been talking about vacation too. Dan called Grandma and Grandpa to see if they had any interest in going away, and they wanted to join as well. In a matter of minutes, we rented a five-bedroom house in Newport, Rhode Island for a full week. We'll be leaving in two weeks! We quickly went from isolating ourselves to inviting family into our home to going away together. It was all done very hastily, which is unlike any of us.

I hope we made the right decision. We didn't spend a lot of time considering the downsides. But the fact that we all committed to the trip so quickly tells me that we are all desperate to get away and need this change of scenery badly. Of course, I hope we don't sacrifice our physical health in the process. We're all committed to isolating before we go away to minimize that risk. Hopefully, this effort will be enough.

The best part of this decision is how happy everyone in the family has been since making the reservation. Chloe, in particular, has been giddy and grinning from ear to ear. It thrills me to see her truly excited.

COPAP Lesson of the Day

- A fresh reminder that I can't always wait for the perfect moment to take an opportunity. I can weigh the risks and rewards then make the best decision under the circumstances.

Buyer's Regret

Dan and I didn't sleep well last night. We both had buyer's regret. Maybe it wasn't the right decision to book a house out of state ... what if the state winds up on New York's quarantine list? What if Rhode Island isn't as safe as New York? What if a family member gets sick? So much out of our control!

But then I picture my family's joy, and it's hard to reconcile cancelling. Abby is shopping for pool toys. Grandpa is researching Newport. Jonah is researching driving routes. My kids are bouncing around the house with glee. Everyone is planning and is so excited to have something to look forward to. I may have concerns, but I am putting on a brave face and going. I need this. We all need this. We will take the opportunity.

COPAP Lessons of the Day

- The more I mull things over, the more reasons I can find not to act, but the opportunity is still there for the taking, regardless of my fear and negative self-talk.

- As an adult, I minimize my need to play and sometimes rationalize my way out of it, but I (and the rest of the adults in my family) need to play right now, just as much as the children do.

Badge of Honor

We went to the ropes park this morning, and I felt really confident. I even started to consider going on the expert course before the season ends. It was the first time the thought entered my mind. We did our usual routine of starting on the intermediate course, then moving up to the easier of the two advanced courses. At that point, we split up ... Dan and kids to the expert course, me to the more difficult advanced course. This course is my nemesis. The one where I hurt my arm before. I felt confident, though. I knew I could do it.

Things started out well enough. I zipped along assertively, noticing my increasing confidence and skills. I got to the rock wall element, where climbers traverse the wall horizontally. It's one of the most difficult elements on the course, but I had handled it well before.

This time was a different story. I lost my footing and slipped. Thank goodness for the harness, so I didn't plummet to the ground. I did take a hard hit to my left arm though. I was scared but able to keep my wits about me and complete the element. I was hurting, but I knew I would be okay and there was no question I'd finish the course.

Finish it I did, and then I completed another course. I was sore, scraped, and bruised, but, strangely, I felt good. I handled the challenge like a champ. I was willing to put myself out there, risk getting hurt, and deal with the consequences. This was all new for me. I don't remember ever putting myself out there like this before, and I liked it.

The bruise isn't pretty (though it is already quite colorful), but I'm proud of it. I wear it like a war wound or a badge of honor. It reminds me of how far I've come.

COPAP Lessons of the Day

- First of all, I am enormously grateful for my harness and the employee who strapped me in safely.

- The fall was out of my control, but my attitude was completely within my control. My attitude made all the difference in the situation.
- Play can be hard, and that's okay. The difficulty makes the reward so much sweeter.

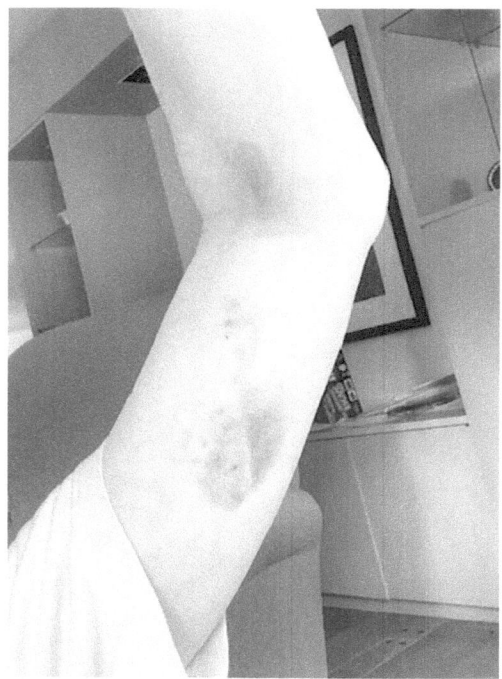

Badge of honor

Safe Ride

Hot, sticky bike ride this morning. I loved it nonetheless. I'm so happy I picked up this healthy habit during the pandemic. I'm also thrilled that I don't get nasty bruises from this activity. While I value challenging myself at the ropes park, it's also a relief to do something that is physically good for me, but doesn't hurt or scare me half to death.

COPAP Lesson of the Day

- Opportunity and growth don't come only from physically daunting activities. Reading, cooking, and bike riding are valuable activities too.

Happy bike rider!

Dog Days

We're dog sitting for our neighbors. The dog's name is Moe. We've watched him before for a couple of quick weekends, but never longer. This time, he's with us for an entire week.

Under ordinary circumstances, I probably would have declined taking care of a dog for a week. Between the responsibility that would inevitably fall on me and dealing with Liam's dog allergies, I don't think our family would have been up to the task. But given the summer we're dealing with, I thought our family could use a four-legged friend to look after. We are embracing the opportunity.

Moe has added distraction, structure, and humor to our unexciting days. Feeding, walking, and playing with him is a satisfying diversion, even when he stymies us by sitting down for no apparent reason in the middle of a walk. He refuses to budge, only to enjoy the outing so much that he refuses to return home at the end of the walk. His presence is a humorous, healthy change for us all.

COPAP Lesson of the Day

- Taking care of an animal gives us an opportunity to care about someone other than ourselves. Hmm...another reason to consider getting a pet.

Good puppy

Taking the Cake

Even though Liam and Chloe don't get to spend a lot of face-to-face time with their grandparents and extended family these days, we've figured out ways for them to have remote fun together.

Today's activity took the cake, literally. The kids taught Aunt Barbara, via Zoom, to bake a pineapple upside down cake. It was hilarious to watch. They walked her through the recipe step-by-step, visually showing her via their screen the steps, the appropriate consistency of the batter, and the proper color.

Lucky for us, their endeavor rewarded us with a delicious, homemade cake. The kids were rewarded with cherished time with their aunt. While Aunt Barbara was, sadly, not rewarded with a scrumptious dessert (her pan leaked all over her oven, which we got a full visual of thanks to Zoom), she was compensated with treasured, uninterrupted time with Liam and Chloe.

COPAP Lessons of the Day

- We can't control the distance or the pandemic, but we can still play and have precious time together.

- At a time when we can't see family in person, I am tremendously grateful for technology. (Oh, computer, I'm sorry I yell at you so often!)

Baking with Aunt Barbara

Tiny Pegs

I sometimes wonder if I'm writing too much about my ropes course experiences. But then I consider that the ropes park has played an outsized role in my efforts to build my resilience, so it makes sense to play an outsized role in my writing.

Today at the ropes course I was more anxious than I'd been in a while. I guess my slip last week took more of a toll on my emotional self than I'd realized. I did fine on the intermediate course, but was nervous, REALLY nervous, to go on the advanced course, even the easier one where I didn't get hurt. Usually, after finishing the easier course, I feel good and ready to step up to the tougher course. Not this time. Nope. It's strange how emotions work. I never know what to expect from them. Just when I think I've mastered how I will feel about something, my mind throws me for a loop. I suppose the lesson is to stop expecting and just go with the flow, let go of the things I can't control. But, please, that's so hard to do.

Despite my fear, I knew I would do the harder course, there was no question in my mind, but I really didn't want to. I was so scared. I was stiff and shaky, not exactly how you want to feel on a thin wire 25 feet off the ground.

And that was before I got to the climbing wall where I slipped last week. I started to cross the wall, slowly and carefully, eyeing each hand and foothold before reaching for the next one. I cheated a bit by clinging with one arm to the wood panels holding up the hand and footholds, but this didn't stop my foot from starting to slip off the teeny nub of a foothold. I caught myself before slipping too far, and my foot found the foothold again. But my heart skipped a beat (or two, or ten). I had to stop, regroup, and talk to myself before continuing. It's a short rock wall, but it felt miles long. Step by step, I made it across. Hallelujah! I did it. I was shaken but happy with myself.

I spotted Dan and the kids on their expert course across the way. I shouted to them, with a big smile on my face, that I'd made it across the rock wall. They enthusiastically shouted, "Yay!" back to me. They gave me enough confidence and energy to continue on. Cheerleaders can make all the difference.

I made it through the rest of the course, shakily and with trepidation, but I finished it. Accomplishment trumps fear every time.

COPAP Lessons of the Day

- I realized today that overcoming challenges and struggles in front of my children is a valuable learning opportunity for them. I sometimes hesitate to let them see me in difficult moments, but I now understand the benefit to them of seeing me vulnerable, scared, and challenged. They get to see me working hard to overcome difficulties and then celebrate with me. What a great lesson for them to learn. I'm living my purpose of teaching without even realizing it.

- I am so grateful for the support of my family. I don't think I would have had the wherewithal to even try this amazing growth experience without them.

The Giver of Pain

Today I had an appointment with my endodontist, aka root canal specialist, aka Giver of Pain. My sore tooth is feeling exponentially worse than it felt before getting the temporary crown, which, again, was meant to decrease the discomfort. So much for that.

The endodontist confirmed my fear. I need a root canal. She recommended I get the procedure done this week and, lucky for me, she could squeeze me in tomorrow afternoon. Yikes. This root canal will be my fourth one. I've been told by every dentist and other mouth doctor I've had the pleasure of seeing that I have beautiful teeth and excellent oral hygiene. Yet, I continually have issues. The dentist, the endodontist, no one knows why I wind up with so many tooth problems. It's emotionally frustrating and physically uncomfortable. I brush, I floss, and, still, I can't control the outcome.

COPAP Lesson of the Day

- I know I can't control everything, but it seems ridiculously unfair that I do everything I should, and things don't turn out the way I'd like. Another life metaphor, I suppose. What I can control is when I get this thing done. Tomorrow is the day, and I look forward to it being over.

Room of Doom

Today was quite the day. Highs, lows, and everything in between.

I spent the first half of the day working. I'm busy this week. Yay! I was nervous about the root canal but happily distracted.

At 1:00, I sent off a PowerPoint presentation to a client, then headed out the door with the family. Why were we all going out in the middle of a Tuesday? We had a family allergist appointment.

Chloe is still desperate for a pet. Since visiting guinea pigs at the pet store, we have contemplated a variety of other options. We thought about a turtle but learned they can carry salmonella. We considered a bunny but heard they smell. A friend recommended a bearded dragon, but we'd have to feed it live insects and rodents. No way.

So, guinea pigs remain at the top of our list. With Liam's significant allergies, our doctor strongly suggested we get him tested to avoid the heartbreak of having to return a pet once it became a part of our family. Dan and Chloe have a bunch of allergies too. I have a few as well. We thought it best that we all get tested.

So, today was the day. We held out our forearms and got a variety of allergens pricked into them. While we all wound up with some puffy, itchy spots, none of us, it turns out, is allergic to guinea pigs or hay mold. Rejoice! We are getting a pet.

Chloe could barely control her excitement. She was elated, feeling sheer glee, and I was elated to see it. She needs this more than the rest of the family. She has been through more in the past two years than any child should, and these last few months of isolation have been very hard on her. She needs something to be excited about, something to love and care for.

Lucky for her, guinea pigs are social animals and should not live alone. So, we'll be getting two of them. Double the love.

So, half our afternoon was spent masked up in a doctor's office. Not exactly where I'd like our whole family to be during

COVID, but we needed to take care of this task for our family's mental health.

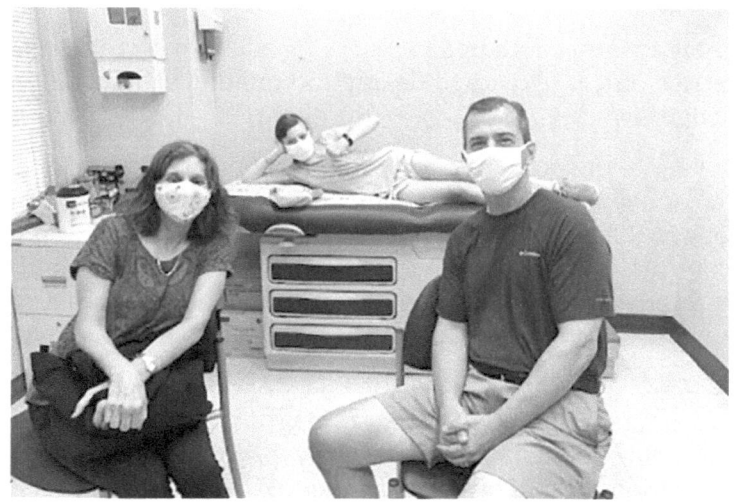
Thumbs up from Chloe!

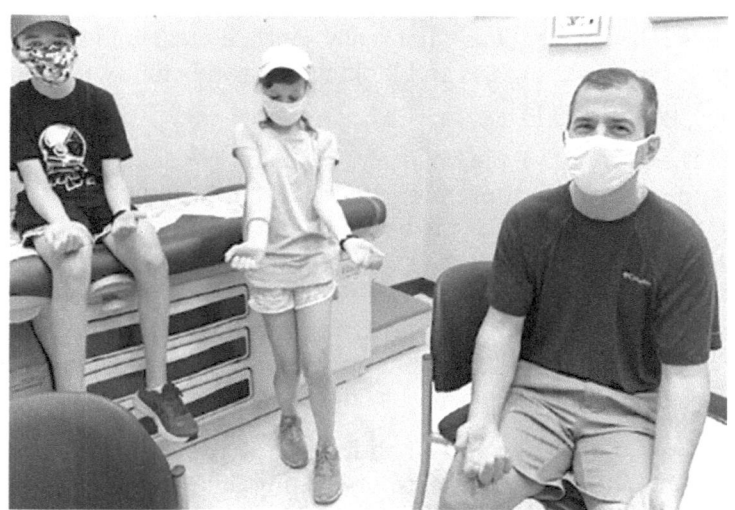
Arms pricked, we anxiously awaited the results

We left the doctor's office at 3:00, with plenty of time for me to get to my 4:00 root canal appointment. An entire afternoon of being in doctors' offices. I'd rather have a root canal. Ha, ha.

My anxiety continued to rise as I made my way to the endodontist's office. I breathed deeply and mindfully, but, still, I was on edge.

I got to the office and took out my phone. I decided I'd listen to an audiobook to pass the time and keep my mind otherwise engaged. I started *Eat Pray Love* yesterday in preparation for today's appointment and was looking forward to continuing to listen today. A divorced woman's story about traveling around the world and learning about herself along the way ... it sounded like a good distraction.

After a few minutes in the waiting room, I was called back to a procedure room. I walked nervously down the hall and into my room of doom. I sat down in a procedure chair, encased in plastic, and stared out a large window. This window would become my calming center. While I enjoyed my audiobook, watching large clouds roll slowly by was what really soothed me. I felt like a kid in a park, lying in the grass and looking up at the clouds, imagining what they resembled.

The doctor gave me Novocain, LOTS of Novocain, and the pain disappeared. Then the drilling began. It's not the noise that gets me, it's the smell. I hate the smell. I tried to listen to the protagonist of my audiobook eat her way through Italy, and had to turn up the volume to compete with the drill. I was feeling complete sensory overload. The sounds, sights, and smells surrounding me were overwhelming. I tried focusing on breathing and relaxing my muscles; it required enormous concentration.

After almost two and a half hours, the procedure was done. Phew, I made it. Of course, this was only Step One. Step Two of the root canal will take place later this month. I'll have to work up my nerve again.

Meanwhile, today was Papa's birthday. I returned home from my procedure to my family eating dinner in the backyard. Luckily, the weather was delightful, so the celebration could take place outdoors without an issue. What are we going to do once the cold weather sets in? Who knows? Another question whose answer we will have to ponder as the months of COVID wear on.

As for me, I was not in a celebratory mood. The Novocain was starting to wear off, and I was starting to get uncomfortable. After a short visit with the family, I retreated indoors with my icepack to let my body and mind recover.

COPAP Lessons of the Day

- I couldn't control the procedure, but I was able to take steps to control how I managed the anxiety it provoked. By taking matters into my own hands where I could (looking out the window, controlling my breathing), I was able to see that I wasn't entirely helpless in a difficult situation.

- Though play is important, sometimes I don't feel like playing, and that's fine.

Absence of Feeling

A root canal is a very strange phenomenon. It leaves you with absolutely no sensation in the tooth. After all the pain and sensitivity, it's a strange thing to hold ice cream or hot tea over the tooth and feel nothing. It's a complete absence of feeling.

When things hurt badly, emotionally I mean, sometimes I wish I could experience a complete absence of feeling. It would be a lot less painful than the fear, hurt, sadness, and confusion I do sometimes experience.

COPAP Lesson of the Day

- Emotional feelings can be hard, and, unfortunately, I can't just have them removed like the nerves in my tooth. I think my best strategy is to realize I can't always control them so just identify them, accept them, and be patient with myself. They will go away ... eventually.

Something Blue

The kids were grumpy this afternoon. I had work to do, and they were annoying (sorry, my loves), so I needed them to be busy. I came to the rescue with a scavenger hunt. Okay, not so brilliant, but the twist was to take a picture of each item they found. Carrying around a phone as they ran through the house and yard made the activity exponentially more interesting. Truth, be told, I also made the hunt long and hard. Hey, I was busy and needed some time.

They finished the activity in a much better frame of mind than they started. They also came up with some amusing findings. Something blue? Chloe took a picture of her own eyes. Something that grows? Liam snapped a picture of himself. Clever or self-centered, I'm not sure, but they had fun and moved their bodies, and I was able to get some work done.

We all wound up better for the activity. Success!

COPAP Lesson of the Day

- A little bit of effort on my part can yield big rewards for all of us. The effort is worth it.

No Backing Down

All packed up and ready to go! We leave for Newport tomorrow!

I'm thrilled for this vacation and can't wait to get there, but we've been isolating for so long that the thought of going out of state, to a strange house, with four other people is highly anxiety-provoking.

We're taking precautions ... lugging along our own food, an abundance of cleaning and sanitizing supplies, and our own linens. But these precautions can't stop the unsettled feeling I have about being in a house for a week with four people outside our "core four." Yes, they are my family. Yes, they are being careful. But living with them 24/7 is creating a whole new layer of discomfort. We will be under one roof, interacting, eating, and playing together. Managing the closeness will be a challenge for me.

I'm not backing down from this trip though. We all need it too badly. I know our mental health will be well taken care of by this vacation. We will do what we can to also remain physically healthy.

COPAP Lesson of the Day

- Darn, I can't control everything. But if I don't take any risks, I will go nowhere. I can't accept that for my family or myself.

Thanksgiving Turkey

Today we headed out to Newport, Rhode Island. Ahh, vacation. It took longer than the three hours our GPS promised, but no worries, we made it here safe and sound, with our bikes still attached (precariously) to the trunk.

Our car was so full that Dan declared that the "car was stuffed like it had never been stuffed before." It was like a Thanksgiving turkey. Things were stuffed in every nook and cranny. It's not like we brought much clothing. I mean, we're not planning on going anywhere outside the house. But because we'll be in and around the house so much, we decided we required lots of paraphernalia to keep us occupied ... kites, bocce, a plethora of balls, tennis racquets, and a variety of other accoutrement to fill our time. Honestly, we'll need to be here a month to make use of everything we brought. Ah well, we got it all here, and we are thrilled.

The house is lovely. Clean, modern enough, decent amount of space, and a beautiful yard. Really, it's the yard that makes it. Large pool, lots of blooming flowers, deck with a television (the kids are thrilled with that novelty), big umbrella, fire pit. We couldn't ask for much more.

The moment we entered the house, the kids ran upstairs, put on bathing suits and made a beeline for the pool. I, meanwhile, made a beeline for my cleaning supplies and immediately got to work. As much as I wanted to swim, I wanted even more to ensure the house was safe and clean. I scoured the kitchen and bathrooms, squirted sanitizing spray, and put out fresh linens. Then could I truly relax and begin to enjoy our vacation.

As for the family, Chloe was beside herself with excitement. Liam was pretty darn happy too. The rest of the family was smiling and cheery. I must say, I'm pretty darn happy myself. I'm so grateful for this opportunity to pause.

COPAP Lessons of the Day

So many today!

- While it feels like so much has been taken out of my control, there remains a lot I can do when I really think about it. I just have to look a little harder to find the opportunities.
- Sometimes the opportunity to just "be" is as important as focusing on living my purpose.
- Sometimes play requires a lot of stuff. So what? If we have space, let's enhance the play as much as we can.

Note the goggles to keep the smoke out of her eyes. Genius!

Joy

I went for a bike ride through Newport this morning. First of all, it was a pleasure that the streets here are a lot flatter than in our neighborhood at home. My thighs were grateful. I rode through our neighborhood, past the beach, past the beautiful houses. It was so lovely. I didn't even get lost, which was a glorious miracle.

I came back to the house to swim in the pool. Ahh. Heaven. Such a pleasure to have our own pool. No crowds, no screaming children (except my own), no fighting for chairs. I don't know if I can ever go back to a public pool.

In the afternoon, Grandma and I went for a walk. We went in the direction I biked earlier in the day. Just as delightful the second time around.

Meanwhile, Liam, Chloe, and Jonah were in the pool for at least six hours today. They were beaming and laughing all day long. That is what this vacation is about, pure joy. Bringing a little bit of peace to our lives during this difficult summer.

COPAP Lesson of the Day

- A day of play with family goes a long way. We're lucky enough to be together for several days, but just one day of pure play is a good start when extended time isn't possible. With so little time together over the past several months, I'd forgotten how rewarding time with siblings, cousins, and grandparents can be.

Just beautiful

Paradise

It's Labor Day! What a perfect day to *not* labor (or be in labor). We rode bikes, sat by the pool, and had a barbeque. Paradise. Nothing more to say.

COPAP Lesson of the Day

- Taking time to relax isn't lazy, it's a smart way to restore myself so I can better serve my purpose and be present for my family. I often forget this little tidbit, but it's important for me to remember it.

Enveloped in Tranquility

I went for an early walk this morning and headed into town. I had to scurry back for a 10 a.m. work call. Ordinarily, I wouldn't be happy about having to work on vacation, but I'm grateful for the project, so it's worth taking a couple hours out of my not-too-busy vacation to do it.

The rest of the day was fantastic. I spent time in the pool in sheer serenity. There's something about water. The weightlessness, the silence, the calm. I get why babies don't want to come out of the womb. The water envelopes you in tranquility. I could get used to this.

Late this afternoon, we headed to the Cliff Walk, a beautiful, miles-long walking path with the ocean on one side and lavish estates on the other. The view was stunning. Little did we know, we were on the rugged end of the Cliff Walk. Rather than simply straight, flat sidewalks, we climbed over rocks. It was natural, rough, and beautiful. We scrambled close to the ocean's edge, watching and hearing the waves crash against the rocks.

The kids loved it, much to their surprise. They weren't too keen on going to the Cliff Walk when we announced we were heading there. We heard some grumbles of discontent. But when we arrived, each of them took off in a different direction, happily scrambling to the water's edge, unexpectedly full of joy. We climbed farther and longer than we'd anticipated because we were all enjoying it so much.

One of the benefits of this COVID vacation is the amount of time we're spending outdoors. Typically, we wouldn't take a vacation with so much biking, walking, hiking, and swimming. But given the circumstances, we don't want to tour museums, go out to restaurants, or go inside anywhere, really. So, with the combination of delightful weather and COVID concerns, we are spending a lot of our time outdoors. And it is truly wonderful.

COPAP Lessons of the Day

- Just ignore kids' annoying complaints when you know deep down the play will be good for them.
- Take the opportunity for a different type of play. An unexpected option may be fantastic.

The explorers

School Days

Today was the first day of school, virtual style. It's all so strange. No meeting teachers, catching up with friends, wearing new outfits, finding new classrooms, or decorating lockers. Just each child alone, with their computer. I'm sad they have to attend school this way, but also relieved they don't have to come into contact with a mass of kids and teachers or sit in poorly ventilated classrooms. There is no perfect solution here.

The good news for us is that Liam, Chloe, and Jonah finished their online schoolwork by 11:30 and were free to enjoy their vacation for the rest of the day. It didn't take long for all three of them to be splashing around in the pool.

COPAP Lesson of the Day

- I can't control some of the limitations of virtual school, but I can be grateful for the opportunities virtual school is providing. When else would we be able to be on vacation while the kids were in school?

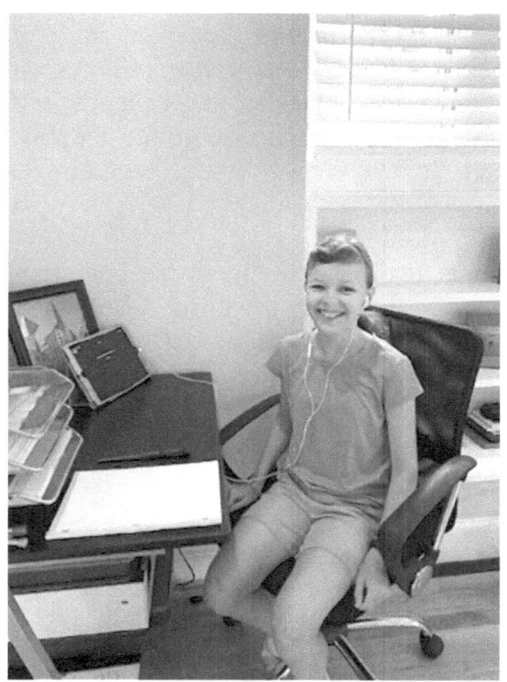

Working hard or hardly working?

Meditation in Motion

I had to spend several hours yesterday and today working. The vacation bliss I'd been feeling wore off for a while, especially last night, when I was troubleshooting a client's technology issues until midnight. But then I thought about the people who don't have the opportunity to take vacation, and I feel grateful and lucky.

And, so, the bliss is back.

I swam laps again. I've decided that I really need a pool in my life. The peace that comes over me when I'm in the water is transformative. I focus on nothing but the sound of my breath, the sight of the bubbles, and the movement of my arms. It's like meditation in motion.

COPAP Lessons of the Day

- Momentary complaints are okay, but I don't want to linger there. I'd rather be grateful for what I have and move on.
- I need to find opportunities to swim. It's so good for me on many levels.

Oh-So-Satisfied

The weather wasn't great today—cloudy and in the 60s—but that didn't stop me from enjoying the day. I swam laps at 9:00 in the morning when it was gloomy and windy out. I didn't care. As long as the pool was heated, I was not going to miss my opportunity. Don't get me wrong, I was freezing when I got out of the water and made a mad dash inside for a hot shower, but my happiness in the water made the chill well worth it.

Next, I read. Laid on the couch with a cup of tea and enjoyed a good book. I even fell asleep for a short while.

Later, Liam and I went for a bike ride. He wanted to get sugar to make homemade lemonade. We hopped on our bikes and took a long detour before running into a store for the sugar.

Late in the afternoon, Chloe, Jonah, Grandma and I went on a hike through a nature preserve. It was calm and quiet and lush. We ran into no one.

I'm sitting in bed now, body tired but oh-so-satisfied.

COPAP Lesson of the Day

- I can't control the pandemic, but I can control my actions, activities, and attitude. I feel good. Really good.

Rugged beauty and my handsome boy

Unplanning

It's the morning of our last full day in Newport. I wish this delightful vacation didn't have to end! I wouldn't say it raced by. It lasted a good, long week. I just want it to last longer.

This trip confirmed how much the family and I needed this break, this escape from reality. The different scenery, change of routine, and outdoor activity are exactly what the doctor ordered.

I still can't believe we managed to pull this off. We booked within hours of deciding to go away and within two weeks of leaving. Not only did we find a house available, but the place turned out to be wonderful. We are all in love with Newport as well as the house. Who would have expected such a successful outcome for a last-minute vacation? Certainly not me.

In my family, we are all planners, like, *serious* planners. Previous trips have been booked a year in advance, with much research, study, and discussion. None of that deliberation happened this time. We had minimal discussion, made a quick decision, and, boom, we were done in an evening.

COPAP Lesson of the Day

- Let go of the control and excessive need to plan! The result of our unplanned trip was just as positive as if we'd arranged it a year ahead of time. I need to remember this lesson. It applies to many areas of my life where I over-plan.

One Last Look

Chloe and I decided last night that we would get up early this morning for one last trip to the Cliff Walk before heading home. We left the house at 7:30 in the cool morning air for a short bike ride to the cliffs. It was refreshing and beautiful, even a bit chilly. We took in every sight along the way.

Once we got to the cliffs, we parked our bikes up against a fence and began our last climb. I breathed in the salty air and took in every view of the rugged rocks and wild ocean. We climbed up the boulders and watched a bird catch a fish and enjoy it for breakfast. We gazed at boats bobbing in the turbulent, white-capped waves. Ahhhh. This moment is what this vacation was meant to be about. Relaxation, tranquility, calm. I soaked it in for as long as I could.

****

We're back home in New York now, and I'm feeling sad. I'm not enjoying the "It's good to be home" vibe like the rest of the family. I wish we were still in Newport. Nevertheless, I'm feeling infinitely grateful for the vacation and the break it provided. The memories will sustain me for a good, long while.

COPAP Lessons of the Day

- Don't leave anything on the table. Take every last opportunity.
- I realized today that my purpose of teaching came through subtly, but profoundly, on this vacation. I taught my children that play is restorative, and they can enjoy a different kind of vacation.

Contentment

Rude Dude

Another Sunday, another trip to the ropes park. No rest for the weary.

I would have been happy to sit this weekend out since we just got home from vacation yesterday, and I got plenty of exercise while away. Plus, I remembered my nervousness from the last time we were at the ropes park, and it didn't feel good thinking about it. But the family wanted to go, so I reluctantly agreed.

I must start the retelling of today's ropes course adventure with the story of a man I'll call "Rude Dude." He wasn't there to climb. He was just standing—with no mask and no climbing gear—in the middle of a bridge in a central area that climbers need to pass over to get around the property. The bridge is maybe five feet wide, no wider. When I came near the man, I questioned him with a simple, "Mask?" He responded, "Yeah, I'm outside I don't need it." I responded, "When you're within six feet of someone you do." His retort? "Then move six feet from me." Wow. Just wow. The property is so large, there is no need to stand smack in the middle of a busy area risking your own health and the health of others, while disregarding the park's strict mask-wearing policy. If you have a reason not to comply, do it away from everyone else.

I was stunned that someone would actually be so rude and so selfish, especially regarding a matter of health. I wish I could say that I shot back with a clever response, but nothing came to me as a I processed what he said. I just walked away, shaking my head, trying to increase my distance from him as quickly as I could, controlling what I could of the situation.

Dan, in all his sweetness, complained to a staff member about this gentleman (and I use the term very loosely) who refused to wear a mask. Dan said he needed to defend my honor. My knight in shining armor (well, in somewhat dull climbing gear, but still ...). His chivalry totally made my day.

As for the actual task at hand—climbing—I got on the intermediate course without issue. I took my time and felt good. Next, we went for an advanced course. The memories of slipping three weeks ago and doing the course while being terrified two weeks ago still felt fresh.

I was nervous, stiff, and jittery. About halfway through the advanced course I decided that after finishing it I would be done for the day. I didn't feel as if I had the emotional strength to get through another course. I wanted to just sit, rest, and be comfortable. I tried convincing myself that I was okay with this decision, that it was okay to take the easier, more comfortable route. Honestly though, it wasn't sitting well with me. I have come so far since starting this ropes course journey. I hadn't backed down yet, and I didn't like the feeling that it left me with. I didn't want to take the easy way out and give up. But, damn, I was scared. These opposing feelings are hard to reconcile. I guess it's okay to have feelings that are at odds with each other. I just have to accept them and then decide if I'm willing to be driven by the feelings that are more comfortable.

Today, I was not willing to let these feelings drive me. I decided I would not end my climbing day yet. I would go right back up on the same course and do it again. I would face my fear and maybe build my confidence.

I'm so glad that I did. By the time I finished the course a second time, I felt less fearful and more confident. I also felt proud of myself for not standing down.

I decided to do the course a third time, figuring the more I did it, the more comfortable and confident I would become. I sailed through the course. I noticed that my mind wandered; I was actually capable of thinking about all kinds of nonsense. Before, my mind was wholly focused on placing one foot in front of the other. But, now, I felt so at ease that my mind was able to go places that had nothing to do with the course ... Rude Dude, floating in the pool in Newport, what to have for lunch ...

Wow, what an insightful experience of how I faced my fears head on. It was so satisfying to pay attention to my feelings, really notice how I coped, and how I succeeded in managing my fears. My analytical mind enjoyed the learning experience.

Maybe next time I'll actually try going on the expert course with the rest of the family. Gulp. I'm looking forward to seeing what learning and insights I'll gain. (Assuming, of course, I survive the terrifying experience.)

As for next time, I'll have to share the results in a different venue. These vignettes and learnings were meant to cover the summer. Now that vacation is over and school is in session, I must end here.

Boy, did I learn a lot about myself this summer. Focusing on building my resilience and taking the time to write down my experiences and learnings has been invaluable for my personal growth. I feel full. Full of life, love, and thanks.

COPAP Lesson of the Day

- It has certainly been a different summer. An interesting summer. Thankfully, a healthy summer for my family. We've all learned a lot and have had to adjust. Are we the better for it? I think so. I know for sure we're not worse off. We have been given an unusual opportunity, and we have lived it for all we're worth. We cooked, we climbed, we biked, we vacationed, we spent valuable time together. Not bad for a summer that forced us to skip most of what summer usually entails and made us change our expectations of what summer should be. While I'm hoping next summer will be more of what we would consider normal, I'm not regretting one bit the adventures and learning opportunities this pandemic summer afforded my family and me. We experienced joy and built our resilience during a difficult time. What more could I ask?

Sacred Summer

A happy ending

Afterword

It is now December 2020. Unfortunately, COVID continues coming on strong. A new strain has emerged. Death counts are up. Several zip codes in my area are in a "Yellow Zone." After our schools opened in October for hybrid learning, they were closed again by mid-November and remain all-virtual.

At this point, vaccines appear to be close, very close, so I remain hopeful that the pandemic will be a thing of the past within the next year.

What's up with my family?

Grandma, Grandpa, and Abby all came down with COVID recently. Thankfully, they are all recovering, but our family experienced a few scary days.

In October, we decided to send Liam and Chloe to school twice a week for hybrid learning. It was an agonizingly difficult decision, but we made it because they needed in-person learning for their mental health. They loved being in their school buildings and seeing friends for as long (well, short) as it lasted.

Dan, Liam, and Chloe have continued going to the ropes park weekly. I, unfortunately, pulled an abdominal muscle (major ouch) on the Leap of Faith of all things, so I never made it to the expert course and have had to take a hiatus until next season.

We continue cooking and baking. Our next family competition is a gluten-free, dairy-free meal. Hopefully, it won't be a taste-free meal.

Chloe has taken up trombone. An interesting (and loud) choice.

Liam has taken up Minecraft. An obsessive (but quiet) choice.

And, we've added two new members to our family. Guinea pigs! Daisy and Lily have provided all of us some smiles and entertainment as the weeks of COVID have worn on.

As for me, I still bike ride when the weather isn't too cold. I continue working on building my resilience, finding family activities, and maintaining my sense of humor as the family buzzes around and brings me joy.

Lily protecting her sister, Daisy

Helpful Links

www.sacredsummerbook.com

Find free resources for building resilience and keeping your family busy, read our blog, and see our summer in color!

www.diligenciatalentconsulting.com

Find training, coaching, and other resources to help build resilience, professional skills, and leadership skills.

www.gf-goodness.com

Order scrumptious, homemade, gluten-free cookies from Liam. His entrepreneurial endeavor supports St. Jude Children's Research Hospital.

For questions or additional information, please reach out to risa@sacredsummerbook.com.

Family Activity List

Looking for fun activities to do with your family? Here's what kept us busy over the summer.

Camp Night

Barbecue hot dogs and hamburgers, grill corn, make s'mores, and tell ghost stories. If you have a tent to sit in, even better! It rained on our camp night, so we brought the fun indoors (including the tent).

Caption Contest

Find a funny picture and challenge friends and family to come up with their best caption. We did ours by email and made sure everyone on the list was copied on the responses so we could all see each other's funny answers. You can find funny photos here https://www.rd.com/list/funny-photos/.

Cooking Competition

There are so many ways to do this…pick a meal (breakfast, dinner, dessert, etc.), a theme (gluten-free, meatless, dairy-free, etc.), a cuisine (Asian, Mexican, Middle Eastern, etc.), or specific ingredients to include. Then divide up into teams and see which team cooks the best meal. We came up with a rubric in an effort to judge each other fairly. Side effect: We ate very well!

Crossword Puzzles

It's hard to create a crossword puzzle from scratch. Do not fear! There are several resources online to help you design a puzzle. They even suggest clues that align with your puzzle. Check out https://www.crossword-compiler.com/.

Debate

Pick two debaters, select a topic, and randomly assign the pro and con positions. Establish ground rules (i.e., five minutes to share your position and an additional two minutes for a rebuttal). We also came up with a rubric in an effort to judge each other fairly. Allow debaters time to research the topic and prepare their speech. For the actual debate, feel free to set up make-shift podiums. We used music stands. Check out https://parenting.firstcry.com/articles/20-good-debate-topics-for-your-kids/ for ideas.

Fruit/Vegetable Picking (then cook or bake with your bounty)

Get out and pick something! Get some fresh air, expend some energy, and see where food comes from. Then look up recipes, make something, and eat it!

GISH

This organization holds hilarious hunts throughout the year. In the process, they raise money for good causes. Check out their website at https://www.gish.com/.

Piñata

Forget papier-mâché! It's so simple to make a piñata out of a box. Determine what you want it to look like...dog? Truck? Taco? Then cover the box with construction paper. Cut out details like tails, ears, etc., and glue them on. You can also use markers to draw specifics. Cut open a flap and stuff the box with candy. When the box is full, reinforce the flap with lots of tape. Poke two holes in the top of the box and put twine or thick string through it. Find a tree, tie up the piñata, grab a bat, and swing away!

Photo Scavenger Hunt

Scavenger hunts aren't too hard to pull together...come up with clues then send your kids around the house and/or yard to find a variety of items (something orange, something squishy, something with fur, etc.). The annoying part is the cleanup afterwards. To avoid the mess, give each kid a phone or tablet and have them take a picture of each item they find instead. Here are two good resources for scavenger hunt ideas: https://www.fatherly.com/

play/scavenger-hunt-clues/ and https://www.letsroam.com/explorer/outdoor-scavenger-hunt-ideas-for-kids/.

Sewing

Whether you own a sewing machine (and know how to use it) or not, your kids can learn to sew. To make a simple pillow, all they need is felt, needle, thread, and some stuffing. For more pillow-making ideas, check out this website: https://mericherry.com/2017/02/17/making-pillows-with-kids/.

Sleepover

A family sleepover is a fun way to spend an entire night together as a family. Whether everyone sleeps in beds, on air mattresses, or in sleeping bags (or a combination thereof) is up to you. Make it special by playing family games, watching TV, and cuddling up together.

Slooh

If your child (or you) likes to stare at the stars, check out slooh.com. With a paid subscription, you can view a variety of space objects through powerful telescopes.

Virtual Cooking

There are plenty of virtual cooking classes out there for your kids (and you!) to learn how to cook. To switch things up, your children can hold their own class to teach others. My kids taught their aunt how to bake a pineapple upside down cake. They sent her an ingredient list in advance then walked her through the steps by videoconference. They also baked then ate cupcakes with friends on a videoconference.

If you or your kids want to learn to cook, we like https://www.baltimorechefshop.com/ and https://homecookingny.com/.

Virtual Game Night

If you look online, there are tons of virtual games like bingo, drawing games, letter/word games, trivia games and on and on. Some are free, some are paid. As long as you provide your virtual guests with a link, you can all play together from the comfort of your own living rooms. Our favorites include https://www.jackboxgames.com/ (paid), https://myfreebingocards.com/

and https://swellgarfo.com/scattergories/.

Virtual Just-About-Anything

If your child wants to learn something new (or *you* want them to learn something new) check out Outschool.com. You can find an unbelievably huge assortment of offerings. I wish I could take some of their classes!

Getting Started on Your Resilience Journey: Applying the COPAP Model to Your Own Life

- COPAP Lesson of the Day Writing Practice
- Learning from Past Experiences
- **C**ontrol: Distinguishing Between What You Can and Cannot Control
- **O**pportunity: Changing Your Perspective
- **P**urpose: Identifying Your Reason for Being
- **A**ttitude of Gratitude: Finding Something to Be Grateful For
- **P**lay: Taking Time to Do Something You Love
- Resilience for Kids: COPA for Kids

Prefer online? Access these exercises and bonus resources at www.sacredsummerbook.com.

COPAP Lesson of the Day Writing Practice

Where do I start?

A. Commit to writing regularly (daily is best) for a period of twelve weeks. It's helpful to write at the same time every day.

B. Write everything about your day – the mundane, special, sad, happy, scary, perplexing. Include your daily experiences as well as your thoughts and feelings about the events.

C. Each day, end your writing with your resilience (COPAP) lessons of the day. One lesson is good, more is fine too. The lessons are critical to your writing practice! It will help you be intentional in building your resilience and allow you to take stock of your growth every day.

Note: While getting started may be challenging, the writing will get easier over time. Once you establish the habit, it will become a regular part of your day. You might even choose to continue writing after the twelve weeks have concluded.

Start now!

My experiences, thoughts, and feelings today.

COPAP Lesson(s) of the Day	One lesson is fine, more is good too!
Control:	
Opportunity:	
Purpose:	
Attitude of Gratitude:	
Play:	

Learning from Past Experiences

Reviewing difficult experiences you faced in the past can help you mindfully manage future challenges.

Name a difficult situation you recently faced.
Ex. *I got divorced 6 months ago.*

For the situation listed above, rate yourself on the degree to which you used each component of the COPAP Model to help you manage the situation:

1 = I did not use the component at all

2 = I used the component to a small degree

3 = I used the component to a moderate degree

4 = I used the component to a high degree

COPAP Component	Rating (1-4)
Control	
Opportunity	
Purpose	
Attitude of Gratitude	
Play	

> **Where you rated yourself a 1 or 2, what specific actions could you have taken or specific behaviors* could you have demonstrated to help you manage the situation more effectively?**

> **What will you do differently the next time you encounter a difficult situation?**

***Action** = something that you do or perform ("what" you do), i.e., reach out to a friend, work out, look for a new job

Behavior = the way in which you conduct yourself ("how" you do something), i.e., have a positive attitude, act with integrity, be respectful

Control: Distinguishing Between What You Can and Cannot Control

Name a difficult situation you are currently facing.
Ex. I just lost my job.

List circumstances related to your situation that you cannot control. For each item beyond your control, determine actions or behaviors* that you can take that are within your control.

Cannot Control	Can Control
Ex. I lost my job	Ex. How I spend my time now that I'm not working, the type of job I want to pursue next, the people I contact about my job search, my attitude about being given the opportunity to try something new

From your list above, commit to 3 actions and/or behaviors* that you will take within the next 2 weeks to maintain control of your situation. Then, identify someone to hold you accountable.

Actions/Behaviors I Commit to Taking	When I Will Start	Accountability Partner
Ex. I will reach out to 2 contacts each day to let them know I am seeking a new position	Today!	My best friend

***Action** = something that you do or perform ("what" you do), i.e., reach out to a friend, work out, look for a new job

Behavior = the way in which you conduct yourself ("how" you do something), i.e., have a positive attitude, act with integrity, be respectful

Opportunity: Changing Your Perspective

Name a difficult situation you are currently facing.

Ex. I just lost my job.

Consider ways to have a new perspective about the situation by answering the questions below.

What sort of freedom has this situation provided?

Ex. I have more time to spend with my family.

What has this situation confirmed or taught you about your values?

What didn't you like about your situation before?

What would you regret not doing now that you are faced with this situation?

What sort of "gift" has this situation afforded you?

What can you do now that you couldn't do before?

From your list above, commit to 2 or 3 actions and/or behaviors* that you will take within the next 2 weeks to see your situation as an opportunity. Then, identify someone to hold you accountable.

Actions/Behaviors* I Commit to Taking	When I Will Start	Accountability Partner
Ex. Because I'm not working, I commit to having dinner each evening with my family	Starting tonight!	My children

***Action** = something that you do or perform ("what" you do), i.e., reach out to a friend, work out, look for a new job

Behavior = the way in which you conduct yourself ("how" you do something), i.e., have a positive attitude, act with integrity, be respectful

Purpose: Identifying Your Reason for Being

No one can define your purpose but you. It is very personal to who you are and whom you want to be in this world.

> Answer the questions below. Please note:
> - You do not have to answer every question. Select those that resonate most with you.
> - Don't pick only those questions that are easy to answer! Pick some questions that make you think long and hard and even make you uncomfortable.
> - For each question you answer, consider WHY you responded the way you did.

What really bothers you?

What brings you extreme joy?

What drives you to get up in the morning?

What allows you to feel peace when you go to bed at night?

What do you want the children in your life to learn from you?

What do you like to read or learn about?

What are you in awe of?

What are you grateful for?
What do people appreciate about you?
Whom do you admire?
Where do you feel most comfortable/most at home/most at peace?
How do your strengths make life better for others?
What can you not live without?
If you tragically died tomorrow, what would you regret not having accomplished?
What struggle or sacrifice are you willing to accept?
What were your passions as a child?

Review your responses above and consider the following questions.

What patterns do you see in your responses?
Which responses make you feel a strong, emotional reaction (i.e., joy, sadness, longing, etc.)? Why did they make you feel this way?

> **As a result of your self-reflection, what do you feel is your purpose at this time?**

Document your purpose.

- Write down your purpose/enter it into your phone/video yourself — whatever works for you.
- Keep your purpose close to you so you can refer to it when you're having a difficult day.

Attitude of Gratitude: Finding Something to Be Grateful For

What difficult situation are you facing?

Ex. I just lost my job.

Respond to the questions below, honestly and thoughtfully.

What are you losing because of your situation?

What are you NOT losing?

What are some alternate endings that could have been worse for you?

What are you gaining from the experience?

What are you learning from the experience?

What can you appreciate about your situation?

What is going right in your life right now?

> **Review your answers above and list at least one thing to be grateful for.**

Document your gratitude.

- Write down your gratitude list/enter it into your phone/video yourself — whatever works for you.

- Keep your gratitude list close to you so you can refer to it when you're having a difficult day.

Play: Taking Time to Do Something You Love

We typically know what we like, but sometimes we could use a good reminder.

Answer the following questions thoughtfully and honestly.
What activities bring you joy?
What do you wish you had more time to do?
What activities have you not tried but would love to explore?
What activities did you enjoy as a child but don't take the time to do now?
Do you prefer doing activities alone or with someone else? Who would be a good playmate?
What gets in the way of your playing?
What can you change to make more time for playing?

Review your answers above and commit to 2 – 3 actions that you will take in the next 2 weeks.

Actions I Commit to Taking	When I Will Start	Accountability Partner
Ex. Going for a bike ride with my husband	Sunday	My hubby

Resilience for Kids

Note: I do not have credentials as a child therapist, psychologist, or psychiatrist. I'm a mom who teaches adults about resilience and have found my tools to be helpful for my own children. Please contact a credentialed professional if you have any questions or concerns about using these exercises with your child.

With a few tweaks, I have found my resilience model to be effective for my children.

When used with children, the model is called COPA. Most of the model remains the same; however, I have changed the definition of the first **P** from Purpose to **P**assion. I have also eliminated the second P. It is unrealistic to expect a child to know their purpose in life; therefore, it is impractical to expect that their purpose can drive them to get up in the morning and achieve their goals. Instead, passion is more appropriate for them to focus on. I ask my children to think about their passions — What brings them joy? What do they love to do? What do they look forward to? — and use the opportunity to pursue these passions to help them get up and going each day. This element is similar to Play in the adult COPAP model.

Following are COPA worksheets with questions I use to help my children build their resilience. Note that these worksheets are designed for parents to work through *with* their children and to start conversations, not to ask children to work through independently.

Questions? Comments? Please feel free to reach out at risa@sacredsummerbook.com.

Resilience for Kids: Control

Control: Separating the Parts of a Situation You Can Control from the Parts You Cannot Control

What difficult or tough situation are you facing?
Ex. I can't go to in-person school because my grandmother lives with us, and she is at high-risk for COVID.

List circumstances related to your situation that you cannot control. For each item you cannot control, determine things you can do that are within your control.

Cannot Control	Can Control
Ex. I have to attend virtual school instead of in-person school.	Talking to my friends by phone, playing my guitar, running, talking to my teachers during extra help hours

From your list above, commit to 1 or 2 things that you will do within the next 2 weeks to have some control over your difficult situation. Then, pick someone you trust to check in with you to make sure you are taking the actions you have committed to.

What I Commit to Doing	When I Will Start	Check-in Partner
Ex. Go running every afternoon as soon as the school day ends to make sure I stay in shape for when I can go back to track practice.	This afternoon	My best friend on my track team

Resilience for Kids: Opportunity

Opportunity: Changing Your Perspective

What difficult or tough situation are you facing?
Ex. My family is moving to San Diego for my mom's job.

Consider ways to change your thoughts about the situation by answering the questions below.
What didn't you like about your situation before? Ex. In NY I have to share a room with my younger brother.
What would you regret not doing now that you are faced with this situation? Ex. Having a sleepover with my friends before we move.
What about the situation is exciting? Ex. I will live near the ocean. Maybe I can learn to surf.
What can you do now because of the situation that you couldn't do before? Ex. Have my own room in our new house.
What could you learn about the situation that would make it easier to handle? Ex. I have never been to San Diego, and I don't know what it's like. I can Google it to see what it's like.

From your list above, commit to 3 things that you will do within the next 2 weeks to see your situation as an opportunity. Then, pick someone you trust to check in with you to make sure you are taking the actions.

What I Commit to Doing	When I Will Start	Check-in Partner
Ex. Google San Diego and my new school	Tomorrow	My dad

Resilience for Kids: Passion

Passion: Identifying What You Love

Answer the questions below. You don't have to answer all of them. Pick those that feel right to you.
What do you love to do in your free time?
When you wake up in the morning, what do you think about doing?
What do you wish you had more time to do?
If you had an unexpected free hour, what would you do?
I feel grumpy if I don't have time to _____.

Read through all of your answers above.
What patterns do you see?
What would you say are your 1 or 2 biggest passions?

Document your passions.

- Write them down/enter them into your phone/video yourself — whatever works for you.

- Keep your passion list close to you so you can refer to it when you're having a rough day. Use your desire to pursue these passions to help you get up and going each day.

Resilience for Kids: Attitude of Gratitude

Attitude of Gratitude: Finding Something to Be Grateful For

Respond to the questions below. Be very honest with yourself.
What difficult situation are you facing?
What are you losing because of this situation?
What are you NOT losing?
How could this situation end differently that could be worse for you?
What are some positive things you are gaining from this experience?
What are you learning from the experience?
If a friend were going through this experience, what would you suggest they could be happy about?

> **Review your answers above. Based on your responses, list at least 1 thing to be grateful for.**
>
>

Document your gratitude.

- Write it down/enter it into your phone/video yourself – whatever works for you.
- Keep your gratitude list close to you so you can refer to it when you're having a rough day.

Acknowledgements

So many people helped birth this baby. In particular, I must thank a few dear people:

My husband for simply being there every day for our family and me.

My children for inspiring me and being willing to try my many wacky ideas with a smile on their face (most of the time).

My mom and dad for teaching me that I can do anything I set my mind to (even if I don't always believe it).

My brother for taking me under his tutelage.

My sister for being a role model I look up to.

My in-laws for accepting me as I am.

Without all of you, I'd be sitting on a pile of lemons, no lemonade in sight.

Want to chat? Want to tell us what you think about the book?

We'd love to hear your thoughts, comments, and questions! Reach out at risa@sacredsummerbook.com.

We also welcome reviews at amazon.com and www.sacredsummerbook.com.